COIN COLLECTING FOR BEGINNERS 2023

Easy Beginner's Guide to Learn How to Acknowledge, Value, Preserve and Start Your Coin Collection from Zero as a Fun Pastime or a Profitable Business.

Herman Kerry Banks

E PLURIBUS UNUM
ONE DOLLAR
LIBERTY
IN GOD WE TRUST
IN GOD WE TRUST
2004
2004
ONE CENT

*Copyright ©2023 by **Herman Kerry Banks**. All rights reserved.*

The purpose of this publication is to provide accurate and reliable information about the subject matter and situation at hand.

By signing an agreement with a Committee of the American Bar Association and a Committee of Publishers, the American Association for the Advancement of Science, and the American Library Association.
This text may not be reproduced, duplicated, or transmitted in any form, electronic or printed, without the express written permission of the author. There are no resale rights here.
Using or abusing any policies, methods, or directives mentioned herein is solely and entirely the responsibility of the receiver reader of this information. This material is stated to be accurate and consistent. In no event will the publisher be held liable for any compensation, damages, or monetary losses incurred as a result of the material included herein.
All copyrights not held by the publisher belong to the authors.
The information provided here is meant exclusively for educational purposes and is therefore universally applicable. There is no contract or guarantee of any kind in the presentation of the material.
There is no permission or support from the trademark owner for the use or publication of the trademark. All trademarks and brands mentioned in this book are held by their respective owners, and this document is not linked with any of them.

*All rights reserved by **Herman Kerry Banks.***

TABLE OF CONTENTS

INTRODUCTION TO NUMISMATICS 1

    Why You Should Collect Coins 3

    Making Your Decision on The Kind of Coin to Choose 5

CHAPTER 1: CREATE YOUR COIN COLLECTION 9

    Getting Started 9

    How To Begin Collecting Coins 14

    Coin Collecting Etiquette 15

    Rules For Profitable Coin Collection 15

CHAPTER 2: WHAT MAKES COINS VALUABLE 19

    Coin Authentication Tools 24

CHAPTER 3: HOW TO PREVENT FRAUD 29

    How to Recognize Counterfeit Coins 30

    Avoiding Scams: Some Suggestions 31

CHAPTER 4: WHERE TO FIND COINS 33

    Notable Coin Collector Websites 35

Attending Your First Coin Show 36

Etiquette is Important 38

Buying and Selling Coins: Suggestions 39

Best Places to Purchase Coins 39

Selling Coins On eBay 43

Special Shipping Considerations for Coins 46

CHAPTER 5- CARE ABOUT YOUR COINS: PRESERVE, PROTECT, CLEAN, AND STORE YOUR COINS 47

Mint Coins 47

Care and Cleaning of Coins 48

Best Method to Clean Dirty Coins? 49

Cleaning Diverse Coin Varieties 51

How to Safely Store Coins 52

Coins For Collection in Their Cases 53

Protecting Your Collection from Theft and Fire 53

CHAPTER 6: YOU'RE NOT ON YOUR OWN! 55

Common Coin Collector 55

Types Of Coin Collectors 55

CHAPTER 7: EXPLORING US COINS 62

Understanding The Popularity of U.S. Coins 62

Popular American Coins 64

    Washington Quarters 64

    Kennedy Half Dollars 65

    Lincoln Cents 66

    Commemorative Coins 67

    Morgan Silver Dollar coins 68

The Most Valuable Us Coins 69

Today's Valuable Coins in Circulation 73

CHAPTER 8: WORLDWIDE COINS 79

British Coins 79

Modern World Coins 85

    Changes in the Utilization of Coins 85

Early Modern Period 86

Early Modern vs. Medieval 88

Significant Historical Coins Ever Struck...................................90

CHAPTER 9: BEST TIPS FOR COLLECTING COINS.....95

Methods To Improve Your Coin Collection......................... 102

Coin Lingo 106

CONCLUSION 118

Investing In Coins 118

INTRODUCTION TO NUMISMATICS

You hear the word *"numismatics"* quite often, even if you don't always fully understand what it means. It is important to understand what we are discussing before diving into the details and moving on to what etymology is and the key elements of this field.

We could characterize numismatics as the scientific study of coins and their categorization across time. There are a lot of intriguing characteristics of coins that can be researched, dissected, and comprehended. They exhibit more than just aesthetic qualities; in addition to a specific history related to the year and location of manufacture, they also exhibit features of a political, economic, historical, and artistic nature. In other words, a real world with various features is concealed beneath the straightforward metal. Numismatics must thoroughly research and "dig" into the world of coins to fully comprehend and examine them.

The term "numismatics" has a long history that can be traced back to ancient Greece. The term's etymology can be traced back to the Latin "numisma," which was itself derived from the Greek "nomisma," or "currency."

As we've seen, the primary goal of numismatics is the study of the coin in all its manifestations. This sector encompasses a variety of sectors. For instance, it covers the study of banknotes, early forms of currency, and items closely related to coins, such as medals and tokens.

This science focuses primarily on examining these artifacts' metallurgy, appearance, year of manufacturing, and other characteristics.

In this light, it should be added that the development of a true "Numismatics of discoveries" over time has also been made possible by numismatics. certain archaeological locations specialized in those discoveries of coins and other artifacts. However, this constitutes the most dynamic and forward-thinking portion of this subject today. The coin was likely introduced in Lydia between the VII and VI centuries to simplify mercenary payment processes. In Greece, it came to represent the existence and independence of the polis. For a very long time, the ideological and exclusive relationship between the polis and the coin was a distinctive feature of the Greek civilization. Most economic activities weren't yet structured in monetary terms, and other currency types were used in the rest of the world. As the figuration was engraved on the surface of the inferior currency, the oldest coins only have one side impressed; one or more punches mark the opposite side. The two-faced coins familiar to us were created as a matter of course by adding a drawing to the better die.

Most Greek coins from the classical era were silver, widely used in the Hellenic world. Instead, Electrum coins were only found in a few locations throughout Asia Minor. Only during the reign of Philip of Macedon was gold discovered in sufficient quantities to meet the demands of standard coinage. At the end of the fifth century, bronze was first utilized in Sicily and Magna Graecia, where the native population had already begun using the metal as money even though it had not yet been minted. Since ancient times, people have given coin quirks that are not fundamental to its economic function as a means of trade. Greek coins, miniature works of ancient engraving art, are fascinating because of their exquisite beauty.

Roman coins "distributed" the sentiments the emperor wished to convey to his subjects throughout the Empire. The dead were given an obolus as payment for their passage on the Charon ferry. Roman catacombs contain imperial coins attached to the early Christians' tombs. A coin was laid on its foundation to symbolize the commencement of a new structure. Gathering different coins is only one aspect of coin collecting. Collecting involves reliving these story fragments and preserving the History of Man in a tiny metal object. Numismatic collecting is unquestionably one of the earliest types of collecting. The love of coin collecting first emerges during the reign of the Roman emperors. It was another usual practice in late antiquity to use a coin as a pendant attached to a choker.

Humanism, a component of the resurgence of interest in the ancient world, is where true numismatic collecting begins. Francesco Petrarch is credited with founding numismatic studies. His Letters also reveal that he was the first to think of studying coins to learn about the past. The future Pope Paul II, Cardinal Pietro Barbo, was the first significant Roman coin collector. Cosimo de Medici was another outstanding collector. The King Victor Emmanuel the III collection, which was bequeathed to Italy and is now on display in the Palazzo Massimo Medal's area, was the most significant private collection in the previous century.

Why You Should Collect Coins

Many people would view coin collecting as a dull and pointless hobby. The stuff that makes you think of your grandfather, who kept various prohibited hobby objects in the attic or basement. If you do hold that opinion about coins or collectors, I really can't hold it against you, but I respectfully disagree.
I used to believe that, but over the course of around two years, I discovered a lot of reasons to respect and like this dying labor of love. If you are passionate about it and have a budget-friendly interest, there is nothing wrong with engaging in coin collecting or hobbies.

Earn income
Whether you like it or not, coin collecting might be advantageous. Not only do many coins increase in value, but if you attempt collecting and decide it's not for you, you'll probably get all your money back, which is unusual for most investments. Some coins' values will change along with the price of the metal. Fortunately,

metal prices tend to rise frequently (especially in a fragile economy like this).

Rarity/Beauty
You can be seeking the most elusive coins available. These will cost more, but one of their strongest selling features is frequently the rarity of the coins. The rarity of some coins may be enough to bankroll you for life if you are fortunate enough to discover a lost treasure. In addition to rarity, coin collecting also places a high value on aesthetic appeal and design. Some coin collectors define beauty as luster and perfection, while others look for coins with appealing designs or compositions. For instance, the 1936 Commemorative Bay Bridge, a half-dollar, is my all-time favorite coin in terms of design. I've always liked the way the Bay Bridge looks, and this coin has the nicest design I've ever seen, thanks to the polar bear on the front.

Challenge
Some coin collectors merely enjoy the hunt for the "ideal" coin. Any coin can be bought with an unlimited budget. The real issue for collectors is locating that coin at an affordable price. Along with the difficulty of locating the ideal coin, many collectors today also act as modern-day treasure hunters. Just picture yourself using a metal detector while strolling the beach and coming upon many coins worth thousands or more. Despite being incredibly unlikely, it is nevertheless worthwhile to hope for.

Educational
Although you probably would only be aware of it once you were absorbed in collecting, coin collecting may teach you a lot. Researching coins and their origins can teach valuable information about history, politics, society, and culture. Consider the recently released State quarters and Presidential dollar coin programs as examples. Even from these two most recent coin series, much is to be taught.

Metal Composition
Many coin collectors only look for coins to add to their collection with this thought in mind because gold and silver are always increasing in value due to their limited supply in the world. Many

people are surprised to learn that you probably handle valuable coins regularly. Did you know that most American coins before 1965 contained 90% silver? Few individuals are aware of this, and even fewer are sensible enough to keep these coins when possible. Pre-1965 quarters alone had a silver worth of almost $4.00 as of this writing. Additionally, the heavier coins have a higher value, so watch for these to begin your collection.

Spread to Children
If you wish to live in the real world, when your children are adults, paper and coin money might not even exist. Considering this, many parents are content to buy brand-new coins straight from the bank or mint in anticipation of a rise in value from which their kids and subsequent generations would profit. Do not for a moment believe that the value of these coins won't rise over time. Even if we no longer utilize as many precious metals as we once did to make coins, their quality also significantly determines their value. For a relatively small initial expenditure, it is a great investment for your children, even though it won't make them millionaires.

Relaxation
I didn't get it when I was younger, the charm. Not even a bit. I understand the value of "silent time" now that I am older. Searching through your collection, doing an inventory, or seeking a particular item can be peaceful. Hobbies are crucial for decompressing stress and temporarily escaping into your little world.

Coin collectors have been since before the Roman Empire, and they do not appear to be going extinct anytime soon. You cannot dispute the appeal of these arguments, regardless of whether you find it to be a complete bore or a worthwhile undertaking. You can have an entirely different motivation for starting a collection. Give it a try, whatever the circumstance may be. You don't have much to lose.

Making Your Decision on The Kind of Coin to Choose

The temptation to go to the local coin shop and overpay for the first shiny coin you see is strong. Checking out the options is a good starting step, however. Coins from the Bible's time period or earlier may pique your curiosity. Perhaps Byzantine coins or medieval

European coins have left you in awe. The sheer number of possibilities in these areas is staggering.

You might also look at modern United States coinage. Fortunately, you have company. More than 130 million people have purchased coins from the United States Mint in the previous several years. While a consequence, you can look forward to interacting with a wide range of interesting individuals while you build your collection of United States coins. Maybe you're not so much into wearing red, white, and blue as you are into collecting coins from all around the globe. You may assemble a group based on location, religion, size, date, or topic. Even more rapidly than some denim brands go out of style, currency trends emerge and go. Knowing your collection budget can help you prioritize your spending since money is always a constraining factor.

Here are some suggestions for unusual and challenging approaches to coin collecting. Make an effort to compile a set of all United States currency denominations. Coins that most people have never heard of, such as the half-cent, three-cent, and twenty-cent pieces, should be included.

Within each denomination, there is a wide range of unique variants to choose from., you'll find a wide range of variants. Half dollars, for instance, come in a wide variety of designs, such as the Walking Liberty, Seated Liberty, Barber, Draped Bust, Franklin's head, and Kennedy. You may focus on collecting just one denomination's worth of items, or you can expand to include other currencies.

Date collecting is a simple and affordable way to complete a set. For instance, accumulating a half-dollar from every year since 1900 would be a breeze. Instead of spending extra money on a coin with a rare mintmark, consider adding the year's least costly coin to your collection. You will have amassed a number of coins throughout the years in addition to the annual coin.

Collecting coins with every possible combination of date and mintmark is growing more expensive. Rare mintmarks appear on several issues in a set, driving up the cost of collecting the set as a whole. If you don't have a considerable amount of money, don't bother trying to complete a collection of Barber dimes. Except for the exceedingly rare 1894-S, which would cost you at least $1 million, you have a good chance of finding and purchasing every date in the series. Alternatively, it is possible to finish many series without going into debt. The Barber half-dollar set may be more affordable than the Barber dime set. Each date and mintmark are available at a reasonable price, and the coins themselves are bigger.

There are many collectors who want to amass the whole set of coins from their birth year. You should collect all of the government-issued mint sets, proof sets, and commemorative coins issued in the year you were born if you are younger than 50. If you're above the age of 50, finding rare coins may be more of a challenge, but that's half the fun! If you really want to go for it, start a collection of foreign coins from the year you were born.

CHAPTER 1: CREATE YOUR COIN COLLECTION

Getting Started

It is common knowledge that coin collectors have an extensive understanding of precious metals. The reason is straightforward. Numerous coins are composed of silver and gold, and most collectors have handled them. This grants them an advantage. They are acquainted with counterfeit coins, gold, and silver and know the value of silver and gold coins.

You must learn more about bullion coins to improve your knowledge of precious metals. Knowledge is essential. If you understand what a rare coin is and how to determine its value, you will be in a much better position to make investment decisions based on fact, as opposed to habit, market trends, or aggressive salespeople's recommendations.

Since the 12th century, individuals of all ages all over the globe have enjoyed the hobby of coin collecting. Among enthusiasts, coin collecting is known as "numismatics," and there are many interesting reasons to start a collection. One of the cheapest methods to start a collection is by setting aside your spare one-, two-, and fifty-pound coins. In any case, they will never depreciate and can be spent if you tire of the hobby.

Some collectors derive pleasure from holding a beautiful work of art in their hands, where they can fully appreciate its age, weight, and history. For some, coin collecting is much more than a pastime; it is a way of life. Rare artifacts are sought after, sometimes with the aid of metal detectors, and esteemed for their rarity and aesthetic value. This primer on coin collecting will teach you the fundamentals you need to start assembling an impressive collection, no matter what sparked your interest in numismatics in the first place.

Many people get started in the hobby of collecting coins after coming upon an intriguing specimen in their spare change, inheriting an existing coin collection, or otherwise obtaining a small number of coins. Some people think they've found an extremely precious coin and want to become rich immediately. No matter where you start, if you follow this advice, your trip collecting coins will be lengthy and fruitful. Now that you know "why" you should collect coins, here are five easy steps to get you started."

STEP 1: Familiarize Yourself With "Mint Lingo."

Coin collecting has its own lingo, much like any other niche hobby or profession. Here are some basic concepts to help you get going.:

- Coins that are now in circulation are those that have been used in regular trade.
- The purpose of minting commemorative coins is to pay tribute to a deserving individual, group, or cause. These numismatic or collectible coins were not made for general circulation.
- The face value of a coin is its stated value and not its market price.
- The intrinsic worth of a coin is determined by its unique characteristics, such as its age, condition, rarity, scarcity, and popularity among collectors.
- A mint is a factory that makes coins (like the Royal Canadian Mint, for instance).
- Minting refers to the operation of creating coins.
- The total mintage of coins with a certain design.
- Numismatics refers to the study or collecting of cash and coins.
- To study or collect cash and coins is to be a numismatist.
- Proof coins are those that have been given a special, high-quality coating.
- Either a coin that has never been in circulation or one with a dazzling field and relief qualifies as "Uncircultion."

Coin "anatomical" terms
The coin's body may also define certain concepts. Some of the most frequent are as follows:
The **Obverse**, often known as the "heads" or "front," of a coin usually features a national symbol or the head of a notable person.

The **Reverse**: The chosen design appears on the "tails" side of the coin. The term "relief" refers to the coin's field, which is elevated or three-dimensional.
The **Field**: The backdrop (field) of a coin onto which relief is struck. A coin's rim is the elevated area around its periphery.
The rim around the circumference of the coin is the "third side." Its texture may be either smooth or serrated.

STEP 2: Begin Collecting (Yes, Seriously)!

Beginning a coin collection may be done in one of two ways: either by purchasing individual coins that catch your eye or by purchasing a whole coin set.
There are several factors that contribute to a coin's worth to a collector. It's possible that this is because of the item's inherent value. Or it might be because it is made of expensive metals like platinum, silver, or gold. But at its core, coin collecting is about making your own personal history. Therefore, start by purchasing coins that pique your curiosity.

Purchase coin sets.
Coin sets are another option for collectors looking to diversify their holdings. Uncirculated or proof coins from the same mint are included in a mint set. Uncirculated sets may be purchased from almost every mint in the world. These are perfect for people looking for a "starter set" on a budget since they are in "mint" condition. Only the Royal Canadian Mint offers collector's items known as "specimen sets." With a frosted elevated foreground and a lined backdrop, these coin sets are of greater quality (and expense) than uncirculated coins.

STEP 3: Define the Type of Your Collection

As your collection expands, you can start to see some patterns emerge. Perhaps it's the allure of precious metals like gold and silver. Or maybe it's just how it's made. Maybe you have a thing for weirdly shaped or colored coins. By keeping track of these details, you can: Narrow down the objects you want to acquire; Assemble coin sets depending on their characteristics. Organizing your coin collection by kind is not required but may add to the fun and satisfaction you get from the hobby.!

Types of collections for beginners
Some collections of this "type" are shown below.:
- Collect coins from a single nation that were all issued in the same year. You might also collect a coin from each year it was issued, like Canadian silver dollars from 1867 to the current day.
- Regardless of where you call home, it's always interesting to add coins from other countries to your collection.
- Find coins that were produced within a given time frame. Is your interest piqued by the First World War? Accumulate coins from or related to the time of World War I, which lasted from 1914 to 1918.
- Animals, plants, flowers, landmarks, historical figures, fictional characters, and cultural events all provide great collecting opportunities in the realm of design. The outcomes might be endless!
- Elements of metal: Try amassing a collection of copper, silver, and gold coins, among others.

Be flexible!
When coin collecting, have an open mind at all times. Why? Perhaps you've developed new passions since you first started out. For instance: Let's say you choose to start your collection with the First World War. After some time has passed, you could decide that only military aircraft technology is worthy of your collection. You may have started out collecting gold coins in general but have subsequently narrowed your focus to those issued to celebrate a certain anniversary or landmark, such as Canada's 150th.

STEP 4: Create Your Toolkit

To start coin collecting, you need just invest in some somewhat pricey equipment. However, there are a few necessities for the safekeeping and care of your coins so that you may get the most out of your experience as a newbie collector. Keep in mind that the more serious you get about coin collecting, the more specialized materials and equipment you will want.

Nonetheless, this is an excellent starter set:
- The smallest details on coins can only be seen with a magnifying lens (preferably 7x magnification).
- A journal, index cards, or software: To keep tabs on how quickly your collection is growing.
- To prevent damage from environmental factors like humidity and dirt.
- Cotton gloves are ideal for handling your cash.
- A beginner's guide to coin collecting that covers the basics.

How To Begin Collecting Coins

With such a vast selection of coins, it can be intimidating to begin a collection. Before purchasing coins, acquire as much knowledge as possible about them. Begin with the loose change in your pocket and familiarize yourself with its components, inscriptions, images, material, and coin type. Once you have mastered the fundamentals, you can determine the optimal method for assembling your collection.

Typically, collectors specialize in one of four primary categories. Collecting by theme is likely the most common way to get started in numismatics; there are countless possibilities. Select a subject depicted on a coin, and you're off and running. It could be a fictional character, a celebrity, an animal, a car, a train, flowers, a building, a landmark, a sport, or a sporting event. The Olympic Games is the most popular theme for coin collecting worldwide, closely followed by football and military history.

Historical significance
Coins from a specific period are a popular collectible amongst historians. You may be interested in a specific period (such as World War II from 1939 to 1945) or year, such as England's World Cup victory in 1966. You could acquire each coin issued yearly, from the Crown to the Farthing, before moving on to the next year. Collecting coins with various mint marks is also an interesting collection method.

Class or designation
Collecting based on a coin's value, you can acquire every major minted design, including those on the Penny and Farthing. Or you may wish to collect all-year varieties or various mint marks.

Nation of origin
Collecting coins is an excellent way to discover the culture and history of a country. British coins are very popular, but those issued in Canada and the United States provide valuable insight into their Presidents and historical periods, such as the Gold Rush, Civil War, and Wild West.

Coin Collecting Etiquette

Keeping care of your coin collection is not only about how it looks; doing so is essential if you want to keep its worth intact. Here are some tips for maintaining their "mint" state.
Wearing cotton gloves is a must while dealing with money. Wear cotton gloves at all times while dealing with money. Coins are easily damaged by the powder or lubricants found on latex or plastic gloves.

Employ caution when handling
Pick up coins by their edges, between your thumb and fingers. Never put your fingers on a coin's obverse or reverse! Are you afraid of dropping your currency and having it go lost? Keep it elevated atop a big, fluffy towel. Meanwhile, try to keep your mouth shut when you're dealing with money. Why? Due to the fact that even a single drop of saliva may leave a permanent mark despite its microscopic size.

Safely store and display
For those who are collecting coins of lower value, acid-free paper sleeves, envelopes, tubes, folders, or albums may be used to store and show the coins. A tiny PVC-free plastic bag or "slabs" (sealed, rigid plastic cases) are recommended by experts as you add more precious coins to your collection. It's also a good idea to protect your investment from loss due to theft, fire, or flood by purchasing appropriate insurance.

From pastime to passion
If you're looking for a hobby that can last a lifetime, consider starting a coin collection for yourself or a loved one. It's true that every interest has the potential to become a serious hobby or perhaps a lifelong avocation!

Rules For Profitable Coin Collection

If you don't take the time to study the ins and outs of coin collecting, you're going to be very disappointed. This will become abundantly clear, especially when a seasoned dealer or collector investigates (and, in all likelihood, rejects) your hasty, uneducated purchases.

There are a few guidelines that coin collectors should keep in mind at all times. Here are five of the most important:

Education
The finest coin collectors are those who devote considerable time and energy to mastering numismatics. They don't only focus on coins but also on the dynamics of the market. If you want to understand more about coins, I recommend buying and reading as many books as you can get your hands on. Catalogs specific to your field of study might enhance these works. A serious collector could even compile a pricing guide for his particular interest.

In addition, numismatic publications like Coin World and Numismatic News are recommended reads for novice collectors. If you're interested in numismatics, you should join the American Numismatic Association so you may borrow books from their library. Connect with other collectors over the phone or online and build lasting relationships. Feel free to inquire as well.

Specialization
Without a plan or a budget, it's tough to get started collecting coins. As someone who is interested in the subject, I find that taking a more "micro" rather than "macro" approach is more fruitful. You may have 52 different problems in your "world of focus," for instance, if you start collecting Charlotte gold coins. A clever individual who is willing to put in the work could probably learn the basics in around two years.

To become as knowledgeable on a much broader topic (say, all gold coins struck by US branch mints between 1838 and 1907) would need a lot more time and effort on your part. Making better purchases is much easier if you have the information to compete with vendors.

Patience
Today is a time when people expect everything right away. It's common for novice collectors to want to rush through completing their sets. The best coin collections were painstakingly assembled over decades. It is feasible to amass a large number of rare coins in a short period of time. Rare are the circumstances in which one could

be able to get rare coins. The beginner collector should not give in to the urge to buy the "wrong coin" because he needs it immediately. In the long run, hasty choices almost always cost more than expected.

Connections
Many serious collectors, it amazes me, rely on newsletters, coin journals, and coin brokers for their "most accurate" information on price, market circumstances, and future trends. In addition to being utterly prejudiced, this data is often out of date. (Keep in mind that dealers have a vested interest in what they are pushing when they publish newsletters endorsing certain coins.)

One can only get reliable data on the coin market from a dealer or collector who often attends exhibitions and auctions. This is due to the fact that the majority of coin brokers and marketers have their knowledge diluted by their superiors before relaying it to the public. If I want to keep working with respectable customers, I have to tell them the truth. On the other hand, I will not give out this information freely to any "tire kickers." The best way to get reliable information is to have a close working relationship with an established dealer.

Behave like a collector
Someone who invests in numismatics without a true passion for the field is nearly certain to lose money. In contrast, most collectors who stick to collecting "pure" items end up financially successful. This is because their motivation for buying coins is pure: they care. After doing significant studies, they only buy things that really interest them. For instance, they know that a coin similar to the one they just bought went for 10% more at a large auction.

They realize that even at the height of a promotion, they are not paying a premium for coins. They aren't buying coins because some voice on the other end of the line instructed them to or because that person guaranteed a 50–75% gain in value for their new coins over the next three years. Perhaps the most crucial of these 10 guidelines is this one: You may increase your enjoyment of collecting and your chances of generating a profit on your purchases by adopting the mindset of a serious collector.

Connoisseurship

As far as I'm concerned, connoisseurship is the ability to identify true excellence within a certain domain. A numismatic expert can tell which coins are the most aesthetically pleasing and stand out from the crowd by comparing them to "typical" examples. A real gold coin, for instance, will have a deep, "crusty" color that will appeal to a numismatic expert. He knows deep down that a coin doesn't have to be big and dazzling to be valuable if it's 150 years old. A refined palate is a natural gift. Either you were born with the capacity to judge what's "best," or you didn't. If you are not a natural connoisseur (and very few people are), you should contact a dealer to help you make your purchases. Less than 5 percent of coin collections are of "connoisseur quality," and they usually see the greatest price increases over time.

Obtaining a Grade

Millions of dollars are spent by people who have no idea how coins are graded on rare coins. Dealers and third-party grading services have their full confidence. This mindset just doesn't make any sense to me. If I don't feel comfortable with my ability to grade a coin, I don't buy it. To give you an example, I think Indian Head half eagles are quite difficult to grade. Honesty be damned, I just can't give grades. How do I fix it? I choose not to buy them.

In a similar vein, I'm confident in saying that I'm an expert in evaluating Liberty Head half-eagles. As a result, I stock up on quite a few of them. Grading conforms to a few simple rules.

First and foremost, it's crucial to look at a wide variety of coins. The best way to learn about coins is to visit auctions and events dedicated to them. Second, I would sign up for a grading class at the American Numismatic Association's Summer Seminars. Third, if I had to pick, I'd focus so that I'd have to learn to grade fewer different kinds of coins. As a fourth step, I would make an effort to consult the coin dealer(s) from whom I make the majority of my coin purchases for guidance on grading. Finally, I would keep in mind that although outside evaluations might be helpful for beginners, personal experience will always win out.

Thinking Long Term

Metals are a horrible short-term investment. Buying coins at a respectable "retail" markup still costs you an extra 10% to 20%

above the going rate on the wholesale market. In order to recoup your investment, the price of the coins you buy will need to rise by at least 10% to 20%. Back in the 1980s, when people were telling you to buy coins as an investment, three to five years was the accepted norm. Ideally, you should keep your coins for at least 10 years, but twenty is much better. It took fifty years or more for the finest collections (Eliasberg, Pittman, Norweb, etc.) to be compiled.

Not Quantity but Quality
Let's say you're allotted $20,000 a year to spend on coins. Four or five beautiful $4000–$5000 coins every year is preferable to twenty $1,000 coins. Quality will be much more important in the future coin market. High-quality coins will be harder to come by, driving up their price. In the long run, it makes sense to invest in the finest coins you can buy. A different dealer had an ad campaign a few years back in which they effectively said that your whole collection had to fit within a PCGS shipping box (that is, twenty coins). His concept was never widely adopted despite its merits. A modest collection of extraordinary coins is preferable to a big collection of mediocre coins, in my opinion, if you are a "generalist" buyer rather than a "specialist.".

Purchasing the best based on your ability
Do not buy anything for more than $10,000 if you are a beginner collector with minimal knowledge of coins and the coin market. It's best to ease into the market gradually over the course of three to six months. When your self-assurance grows, you may put more money into the coin market.

CHAPTER 2: WHAT MAKES COINS VALUABLE

Do you ever think about the monetary worth of coins? Right from the start, we can tell you that the solution is not always simple. A coin's worth may be affected by a wide variety of things. While it's exciting to see a coin that "resembles" yours selling for tens of thousands of dollars online, you shouldn't get your hopes up too high. Sometimes, the value of your specimen will be higher than average.

Why are coins valuable to begin with?
Coins are a form of currency. They are currency. Historically, a coin's worth was directly proportional to its metal content. At now, coins are only worth what the government thinks they are worth. "Fiat money" describes this kind of currency.
Gold and silver bullion coins from antiquity and the current day are both highly sought after. In most cases, their true worth much exceeds their face value. In addition, certain coins may gain in value as collectibles.

The Seven Elements That Determine a Coin's Worth

Consequently, what variables predominate in establishing a coin's worth? Take into account the following factors:

1. Mintage
One of the primary variables of a coin's worth (beyond its date and mintmark) is its mintage. The number of coins that were first produced at the United States Mint is indicated by the mintage number. There are often more collectors than coins available if the mintage is low.
The mintage is one aspect of determining a coin's worth, but it is not the only one. The number of coins struck does matter. It gives the maximum number of coins that might ever exist in circulation. Many coin collectors, however, place too much emphasis on mintage figures rather than the coin's population estimate.

2. Population Estimates
Approximate numbers are more common than precise ones when estimating a population. In other words, it limits the total number of

that currency that may be in circulation (including in museums, private collections, the market, and "wild" circulation).

For what reasons does the general populace have greater weight in setting the value of a coin? There were 44.6 million 1921 Morgan dollars struck at the Philadelphia Mint. There are really a lot less of these coins left than people think. The amount of circulating 1921 Morgan dollars is likely far lower than what the records reflect, owing to losses from theft, fire, burial, and melting.

Here is an even better illustration of the importance of population. Take Saint-Gaudens' 1927-D double eagle as an example. A total of 180,000 were struck, a rather low but still respectable number. However, the federal government melted most of them in the early 1930s, so now, just around two dozen are known to exist. It is estimated that the typical 1927-D Saint is worth between $2,000 and $3,000. However, since there are so few of them left, this coin is worth at least $500,000 on the market.

Another form of the population that matters is the "pop" reports from the two major independent coin grading agencies. These include both PCGS and NGC (NGC). These two businesses disclose accurate figures of how many of a certain coin was rated as a certain grade in their "pop reports."

It's crucial to remember that the estimated population of all coins is far more than the number reported by pop reports. PCGS and NGC's population statistics, however, greatly enhance the estimation of a coin's total rarity, especially for the scarcer coins that are currently on the market.

3. Demand

To find more than a few dozen of anything seems quite rare. Is it unusual, however, for five or ten people to want a coin that has twenty or thirty people still alive on it?

Tens of thousands of serious coin collectors are willing to pay $500,000 for a 1927-D Saint-Gaudens double eagle because they want one so much. In contrast, there are several rare foreign coins, of which just a few remain in circulation. However, you may get them for a song since so few people pay attention to or collect them.

Compare this with, say, a 1909-S VDB Lincoln cent. For years, this coin has been considered by collectors and dealers to be the rarest of the rare. But wait just a second... How many were produced? The United States Mint produced 484,000 1909-S VDB Lincoln cents. How many people are still here? Maybe fifty thousand or more.

How can something with tens of thousands in circulation be considered rare? Digging a bit deeper is required. The laws of supply and demand rule everything. The Lincoln cent struck in 1909-S VDB condition is one of the most sought-after coins in the United States and, maybe, the whole globe. It's quite rare since there are only 50,000 of these famous coins accessible to the millions of collectors who want and can afford to buy one.

It's not as simple as supply and demand when it comes to the 1909-S VDB. The pursuit of notoriety is also a factor. There aren't many coins that are considered rare and collectible outside of the coin-collecting world, but the 1909-S VDB penny is one among them. The 1927-D Saint-Gaudens $20 bill has no such flaws. Only a small percentage of coin collectors are aware of the rarity of this particular piece of gold. The 1909-S VDB cent, on the other hand? Even those who don't collect coins recognize this classic as "the 1909 penny." It's possible that non-collectors won't always see the "S" mintmark or "VDB" inscription, both of which are quite important. (This alludes to the fact that the coin was created in the San Francisco Mint by Victor David Brenner.) The widespread awareness of the 1909-S VDB penny's existence, however, is what makes it such a significant rarity. The more the public's familiarity with a famous coin like the 1909-S VDB penny, the higher its demand and value.

The state of the coin is a major determinant of its worth. It's not only how worn a coin looks that determines its condition rating. It also includes the coin's color, tone, wear, and general aesthetic appeal. The value of a coin is significantly affected by all these factual and subjective elements. Similar to the relevance of mintage and population, the condition is crucial. Coins in excellent condition are becoming harder to find as time passes. This relative scarcity, together with collector demand, leads to price increases. For the most accurate information about a coin's condition, collectors should go to unbiased authorities like NGC and PCGS.

5. Age

While it's not always the case, older coins tend to fetch a higher price. It's not so much becoming older as it is everything that comes with it:

As more of these older coins are lost or destroyed, they become more difficult to find.

Damage and wear are more likely to appear on an older coin. As a result, there are fewer pristine instances of this coin kind. Older coins are usually harder to come by than newer ones. They aren't in circulation and can't be bought from the mint. Therefore, the myth that ancient coins are more valuable than new ones must be dispelled. An essential aspect of a coin's worth is its age and the circumstances surrounding that age. Coin collectors can specialize in a certain year's worth of coins. A coin's collectible value might rise or fall depending on the year it was struck.

6. Design

The aesthetics of a coin may transmit important messages about a country's history, culture, and values. This endearing quality of coinage has been appreciated by many civilizations throughout history. Even the oldest coin illustrations tell us something about the culture and society of the period they were created in. Whether an emperor or natural fauna is shown, the design conveys meaning about the culture it comes from. How would this scenario impact value? Some people are willing to pay more than face value for a coin that has an appealing design. Designs are appealing to both designers and collectors. To round out their collection, they can be looking for a single example of a certain style. Both the debut and demise of a coin's design are commemorated on the coin. Both of these factors contribute to a coin's collectability. In addition, the designs of limited-edition collector coins are often quite interesting.

7. Bullion Content

The term "bullion content" describes the percentage of precious metals in a coin. But what exactly is the composition of the metal in the coin? Silver, gold, and platinum coins are more valuable than their base metal equivalents. All precious metals, such as gold, silver, platinum, and palladium, are integrated. The reason is obvious: the cost of these metals is higher.

Therefore, a gold or silver coin will have a high melt value. On occasion, the term "intrinsic value" is used interchangeably with the term "melt value." How to identify a coin's metal content is the primary issue. Color blindness is not a sufficient criterion. Many coins merely have a gold or silver coating on the outside. Even a metal coin might seem like real gold at first sight. Modern bullion coins make it easier for buyers to do so. Consistently displaying their exact weight and quality markings. Sometimes, extra testing is needed to determine whether or not a coin is made of metal. If you want to learn more about how to spot fake silver, read this article. (The same advice holds true for gold)

Other Elements

Additional considerations in coin valuation include the following:

Inaccuracies: Does your currency qualify as a "coin with an error"? Does the coin, therefore, have a minting mistake? It is not always easy to tell the difference between a mint fault and a coin that has been damaged after it was struck. You should look for examples of errors and evaluate your coin against them. Coins with genuine errors are usually more sought after and fetch higher prices than regular issues.

Provenance: Was a well-known individual the previous owner of your coin? Did you get it as a part of a set? This refers to the background and history of the coin in question. The value of a coin might skyrocket if it has a fascinating backstory.

Coin Authentication Tools

For centuries, people have been collecting coins. The earliest coin collection dates to 63 BC. While technology has altered the coin collection tools available, the fundamentals remain unchanged. Each tool is necessary for initiating and maintaining a coin collection.

Now is as good a time as any to begin researching the next generation of coin tools and collecting materials if you want to climb to a higher level of coin collecting in the near future. As your coin-collecting expertise and confidence have grown, you've realized there are more factors to consider and choices to make than just dates, mintages, and varieties.

The field of die variation collecting, for instance, is growing, as are many other subfields of this fascinating and enlightening hobby. If you're a dedicated collector, you may want to verify their authenticity before putting down money for rare or expensive coins. You will need more advanced or complex coin-collecting instruments to help you do this and move further into the world of advanced numismatics.

#1. The Digital/Electronic Scale

For serious coin collectors looking to take their hobby to the next level, an accurate digital scale is a must. This kind of scale can be trusted to accurately weigh and verify coins. This is the single most crucial indicator of whether or not a specimen is genuine. In addition, checking for any mistake coins requires the use of an accurate digital scale.

You might tell whether a recent clad currency from the United States was struck on a planchet from a different denomination of coin or a silver blank, for instance. You'll also need a digital scale that's sensitive enough to measure down to 0.01 grams, regardless of whether you're using grams or ounces as your unit of measure. The price of these accurate scales ranges from $30 to $150.

#2. The Digital Caliper

The diameter of each coin in your collection may be determined with the use of this excellent and important tool, often known as a size gauge. Once the coin is positioned between the caliper's jaws, the jaws are slowly closed until they make contact with the coin's obverse and reverse. Coins that were struck from a collar are of the wide strike kind or may have been struck from an incorrect planchet and will not calibrate to their 'real' diameter. The caliper has to have a resolution of at least 0.01 mm on its digital display, and it may measure in both inches and millimeters for your convenience. Prices for these digital calipers range from $7 to $60.

#3. Stereo Zoom Microscope

This essential coin tool magnifies your coins so you may inspect them with a level of detail unattainable by the naked eye. For the best possible readout of the coin's surface, your microscope should have dual eyepieces and optics. The coin should be properly illuminated by a light source installed in the microscope's neck for the best viewing experience.

The ideal zoom range for a microscope is between 10X and 45X, providing the largest field of view at each magnification setting. To check the genuineness of your coin collection and spot die variants, a stereo zoom microscope is indispensable. The optics of cheaper microscopes are often of poorer quality, resulting in a hazy picture; thus, it is best to spend as much as possible on a good one. High-quality stereo zoom microscopes may be purchased for between $150 and $600.

#4. The High-Quality Digital Camera

When it comes to documenting your coin collection, nothing matches professional-grade digital photographs. When it comes to securing insurance for your collection, this is another must-have item. In addition, you should have a camera that has a macro setting. If you're serious about your photography and want the best results, you should learn more about digital SLR (single-lens reflex) cameras.

Taking photographs of your coin collection, especially with a high-quality camera, allows you to share, study, and enjoy some of your most expensive coins without risking loss or theft by taking them out of a bank safety deposit box. These digital cameras start at about $200 and go all the way up to $1,600 or more.

#5. Coin Lamp

If you want to know the actual color of the coins in your collection, you'll need good lighting. For precise coin grading, a daylight lamp that replicates the sun's whole range of hues and natural white light must be used. Uncirculated copper coins seem redder than they really are in low-spectrum indoor lighting. In comparison, silver coins seem even more brilliant under fluorescent lights. Then determine if a coin has been circulated or not; natural light is preferable to artificial light. The 'Tensor Light' and the 'Ott Light' are the two most common types of magnification used by professional numismatists.

The Tensor brand of light produces full-spectrum lighting with realistic color rendering, much like sunshine. The 110-volt, 13-watt versions have a motorized shade that cuts power when the shade is closed. It is generally agreed that the OTT brand light is the best for coin photography. It has a 10,000-hour lifetime True Color fluorescent bulb and a height adjustment range of 11–19 inches thanks to its movable top. It has impeccable color matching and clean contouring. These light fixtures may be purchased for between $25 and $60.

#6. Coin Cataloging Software

No matter how experienced you are with collecting coins, you know how challenging it can be to keep track of an ever-increasing stockpile, especially if it starts to outstrip your abilities to care for it. Carlisle Development Corporation's The Coin Collector's Assistant is a top-notch piece of software that effectively addresses this difficult issue. Coin collectors will find this program to be an invaluable tool for keeping tabs on, cataloging, appraising, and grading their whole collection of coins. The coins and paper money a collector currently has may be simply recorded, and the coins that are still missing from the collection can be noted, along with any excess or duplicates. Entering, editing, or viewing all coin and money data is simple and requires no technological expertise.

It not only helps you keep track of your purchases, sales, and earnings, but it also shows you the most up-to-date pictures, statistics, and market prices of coins and currencies. Included are current coin values provided by Coin World, the foremost authority in numismatics, as well as a complete database of U.S. coins with referencing by date and mint mark for all coins produced by the U.S. Mint, including all U.S. circulating coins, pre-1954 and modern commemoratives, bullion coins, Hawaiian and Colonial coins, and more.

The Official A.N.A. Grading Guide is the gold standard for coin collectors across the globe, and Grading Assistant is the interactive version of that guide. The United States Mint has been producing several kinds of coins since 1793. More than a thousand examples of each kind are included in this software. You may get this suite of programs for about $140.

#7. Coin Magnifiers and Loupes

Magnifiers and loupes for coins are essential for examining the finer characteristics of coins, which are invisible to the human eye and are thus crucial for determining the authenticity of your coins or determining the variety of coins you have. To grade coins accurately, you need a high-quality coin magnifier to inspect the surface for imperfections and minute features.

When grading coins, the American Numismatic Association suggests using a magnification of between 5X and 10X. Binocular headband magnifiers and handheld coin magnifiers save you from touching your collection as you inspect it. Bar or page magnifiers, extra-zoom insets, LED magnifiers, pocket magnifiers, visor-style mounts for eyeglasses, and flip-up loupes are just some of the options. Prices for coin magnifiers range from $15 to $60.

#8. Gloves and Finger Cots

Gloves are an absolute must for anybody who collects coins. You should avoid touching your coins with your bare hands since the oils and acids on your skin may harm the coins' surfaces, sometimes irreparably. This is especially crucial when dealing with uncirculated coins, which must be kept in perfect condition. Gloves are a must if you want to keep your cash safe from becoming dirty.

Many professionals in the world of numismatics and collecting agree that the most comfortable gloves are those made of soft cotton material. Instead of using cotton gloves, you may purchase powder-free latex or nitrile gloves and finger cots from any coin supply online. Gloves may be purchased for about $2, while latex finger cots can be purchased for pennies.

#9. Coin Tongs
For the sake of protecting the surfaces of proof and mint set coins, coin tongs are an excellent instrument for handling coins around the rim. When cleaning coins or immersing them in solvents or other liquids, collectors should use coin tongs. The plastic covering on most coin tongs prevents the coin from being scratched while providing a secure grip. They cost anything from $3 and $18.

#10. Flat-Clinch Stapler

Stapling may be quite annoying, especially when using coin flips or cardboard 2x2. Use the fantastic Max brand Flat Clinch Staplers, which leave the staples flat and save a ton of room when storing your cardboard 2x2s and flips, to put an end to this problem once and for all. The simplicity of not needing to use pliers to re-clinch the staples, the absence of coin scratches, and the elimination of bent or crushed staples are all benefits of this ingenious flat-clinch closing motion design. This must-have accessory, which typically costs about $38.

CHAPTER 3: HOW TO PREVENT FRAUD

I included a chapter on counterfeit coins and scams when I wrote this book. Their prevalence has increased dramatically recently, and even the most seasoned coin collectors occasionally fall victim to con artists. Experience is the most effective weapon you can employ against cons. Becoming more knowledgeable and gaining experience will make scamming more difficult. However, this is only sometimes sufficient, and you should now begin to understand how to identify counterfeit coins. The overall procedure for producing counterfeit coins is simple to comprehend. To authenticate coins, a specialized device stamps them. Coin forgers have the expertise and training to replicate rare coins that collectors pay a premium for. Most fake coins are made by pouring molten metal into molds, which leaves die marks when the coin cracks.

Experts in spotting fake coins have found that the dates on the ones that have been tampered with are either missing or incorrect. The owner of a suspected counterfeit collector coin might try to reclaim his other coins, which he feels are genuine and of similar worth. He might next examine the two coins side by side to see whether the fake has any distinguishing features.

You can tell whether a coin is worth more than five cents by looking for corrugations around its circumference. The silver coins have very delicate fences. This process is also known as "reeding." Coins that are genuine may be easily identified by their razor-thin edges. If the edges of the fake coin are too thick, it will be easy to see.
The receiver is not allowed to transmit the fake currency back to the sender. It is imperative that he does all in his power to stall the offender. If the person is on the run, he must make an effort to keep eye contact with him at all times. During the conversation, he has to take mental notes on the person's appearance, including what they are wearing and whether or not they are accompanied. Get their license plate number if they have a car, and report them to the police right away.

How to Recognize Counterfeit Coins

There are several indicators that may help you tell whether a coin is real:

Restriking a coin might be used to verify its authenticity. The coins have the same or comparable qualities to the originals, but have an earlier release date from the country that minted them. Ancient coins from one country are sometimes reissued by another. Even though it seems like a fabrication, these documents were legitimately issued in the nation of their origin.
Forgery may be connected to financial gain. This may perhaps be the main reason why the counterfeiting ring exists. During wartimes like World War II, the federal government regularly used forgeries as a tool of political propaganda. Germans made a lot of fake British and American banknotes to weaken their opponents' financial standing. Replica coins are another common kind of counterfeit currency. To create a replica coin, the original is copied down to the smallest detail. However, specialists in the field are able to spot fake coins by looking for certain telltale signs. Some people deliberately stamp "copy" onto currency. Most of these copies are displayed in museums or used in classrooms.

It is widely believed that counterfeit coins are mass-produced in Lebanon. Numerous museums, corporate executives, collectors, and even countries looking for their missing antique coins fell for the con that these coins were utilized. There are two sorts of forgeries—those that are designed for circulation and those that are aimed at collectors—in which the coin is accepted at face value, notwithstanding the forger's illegality and obtrusive, meaningless worth.

Talk to an expert if you want to know for sure whether a coin is genuine. Experienced professionals in this field would be able to spot the fake metal in an instant. A coin collector would have a better understanding of these pieces. Collectors should exercise extra caution around rare, valuable coins, which are the main target of counterfeiters. They go for the most lucrative market they can find.

Avoiding Scams: Some Suggestions

Numerous individuals enjoy shopping online, where fantastic coins can be discovered. Rather than searching for stores selling collectible coins and other mementos, a person may choose to do his shopping from the comfort of his own home because it is convenient and time-saving.

The main difference between an online auction and a live auction is that in the latter, the highest bidder wins. There are many people who like bidding online and who know all the tricks of the trade to come out on top in an online auction. A person may find just about whatever they're looking for to buy online. Many coin collectors shop at this shop to get their hands on the coins they want. Customers may shop around for the best price and make secure payments without ever leaving the comfort of their own homes.

Many purchases and payments are made via this online auction, despite the fact that it may be too unsafe for a buyer to depend on an anonymous vendor. Despite the prevalence of fraud in the current day, many websites that do business online reassure their customers that they have nothing to worry about in terms of fraud. According to their findings, internet fraud accounts for just 0.0025% of all occurrences. Possibly just 1 in every 40 thousand internet purchases is a scam. However, the FBI's inquiries prove that the statistics are erroneous. Their numbers show, they say, that fraud is significantly more likely to occur. The FBI is trustworthy enough to entrust with one's safety. Most internet coin sales are legitimate, but it's possible you'll encounter some shadiness and unpredictability in the transaction itself. There are certain commercial deals that constitute fraud in and of themselves. The Internet presents the largest possibility for fraud, followed by flea market merchants, live auctions, mail-order sellers, and certain coin shops.

A coin buyer should be aware of the term "feedback" and how to use it as a safety measure. Bidders' scores would be shown, allowing them to see how their bids stacked up against the competition. If there is a significant likelihood of fraud based on negative feedback, the participant may withdraw from the auction. Another method of gleaning information is to look for "positive feedback" from members and compare it to the seller's reaction. One can determine what information could be relevant based on the replies. A person needs to be wary of accepting just any bargain that comes their way.

Sometimes people are tricked into buying the merchandise. The online picture showed the coin the customer wanted; however, they sent another kind of coin. It seems like a hoax in these situations. The customer must ensure that the item he ordered is the same as the one shown. Here are some precautions you may take to safeguard your coin search against internet fraud. The online picture of the coin one wants to buy should be saved. After a sale is completed, some vendors hide the product's name and picture.

CHAPTER 4: WHERE TO FIND COINS

Many people got into coin collecting because it was a fun pastime. But you've probably heard (or experienced) tales of folks who cashed in their old coins for a tidy sum. As a result, more and more individuals started their own coin collections. There are several options available to you if you're interested in beginning a coin collection.

Coin Dealers Shops
A small number of store owners are knowledgeable coin dealers who are selling specific coins. These coin shops are essential for learning more about coin collecting and coins. These coin stores may be expensive because they are attempting to profit from selling their coins. If you're well-informed and have a coin expert on your side, you can get fantastic deals.
Individuals who are complete novices should refrain from purchasing from coin shops, as they run the risk of overpaying for their coins. In addition, many owners are not receptive to price negotiations, so you either pay them the asking price or leave. However, if you are a beginner, I recommend visiting them without purchasing to learn more about coins and how they are graded.

Coin Displays and Shows
On occasion, your local mall may include a display of numerous coin sellers. These will let you browse their inventory and buy a few select things at a reduced price as a result of market pressures. Many brand-new coins will likely be available for purchase and perfect for your collection.
These coin exhibitions are incredible and not just for collectors. However, it is also for collectors of rare and difficult-to-find coins. Even if you are a novice, as you probably are, you can still find good deals and people willing to share unique and interesting stories about coins. The primary disadvantage of coin shows is that they are not held in cities. If you live in a small town or city, you may need to drive to the nearest major city.

Mail Orders/Web Sites
Many vendors accept mail-order and other online payment methods (including PayPal) on their websites. You should do your homework

on these firms and study their policies thoroughly to be sure you can return the coin for a refund if there are any issues.

There are likely many fraudulent websites whose sole purpose is to obtain your payment for a single legitimate website. Before paying anyone online, you should request feedback and numerous images and remember not to reveal PINs or passwords.

In recent years, many online coin-related frauds have been perpetrated. Check for the best deals but focus on the specifics. You do not want to be the next victim of fraud.

Flea Markets
Here is not the typical area to look for rare coins. However, these areas have varying conceptions of prices because they are taught different ways to value coins. You might expect to uncover pricey coins, and with any luck, one rare coin will make it all worth it.

Typically seeking a quick sale, vendors at flea markets are likely to offer discounts if you purchase their products in bulk. Attempt to purchase additional items to receive your coin as a reward. Even if you're a beginner in coin collecting, sometimes you know more about the seller than the seller does!

An auction is the greatest venue to buy rare coins for investment purposes. People selling their rarest and most valuable coins are only accessible at auctions. These auctions often take place online, and the vendors typically only accept the highest bids. But you should know that some of these vendors are scam artists that won't provide value for your money. If you're interested in placing a bid on one of these coins during an online auction, you should do some research beforehand.

Notable Coin Collector Websites

The Internet is a fantastic resource for learning about coins and coin collecting. Unfortunately, the Internet is also the largest source of misinformation worldwide. These leading coin-related websites were chosen based on their informativeness and dependability. In addition, you can select from various sites that offer the greatest variety of information and knowledge.

- If you're looking for information about United States coins, go no further than CoinFacts.com. Detailed descriptions and images of colonial, private, and government coins from every year they were produced are provided. Look at these... http://www.pcgscoinfacts.com/

- Coin Grading explains the process of grading coins. Do we all not? The website of coin grader and numismatist Jim Halperin is a great location to begin learning about the hobby. Look at these... http://www.coingrading.com/

- This is the leading currency site on the web, packed with interesting and informative content. Look at these... http://www.coinlink.com/

- National Museum of American History, Smithsonian Institution: Check out Coins, Currency, and Medals by clicking the Collections tab. Beautiful displays of all varieties of American coins may be seen here. The Smithsonian Institution has the biggest and most valuable collection of coins in the world. Look at these... http://americanhistory.si.edu/

- To learn more about the coins, medals, tokens, and paper money of countries all around the globe, including the United States, check out Numisma Link, an informative educational website. Bibliographic sources are highlighted, with the list focusing on websites, numismatic organizations, and world mints. You may use this page as a jumping off point. Look at these... http://www.numismalink.com/

- The Numismatic Bibliomania Society is an online resource dedicated to advancing scholarly study and the collecting of numismatic literature, including but not limited to: auction catalogs; dealer price lists; periodicals; books; and other printed materials pertaining to United States and foreign coins, tokens, and medals; colonial and private United States and foreign paper money; and ancient and foreign tokens and medals. Look at these... http://www.coinbooks.com/

Attending Your First Coin Show

The greatest method to become a knowledgeable numismatist is to visit coin exhibits on a regular basis. It's a great method to get your hands on coins, tokens, medals, and bills. Even though costs may be higher online, some people still choose to do their shopping there because of the privacy it provides. Participating in a hobby community is a great way to make friends and have fun.

Start by visiting a local coin show.
Avoid having your numismatic debut during a regional or state convention, since you will be completely overwhelmed. Monthly coin displays are held by a plethora of coin groups all throughout the United States.

Join a group in your area and start showing up to meetings before you see a show. The group will provide a wonderful opportunity to learn about numismatics. In addition, seeing other club members in the roles of dealers and consumers can put you at ease before going to your first show. To get a feel for the place and its inhabitants, a stroll is in order. Don't rush towards sitting down at a table.

Engage club members before and during the performance.
If you're just getting started in collecting and aren't sure what to focus on, ask other collectors for tips on reputable dealers. There is a wide range of options for those interested in numismatics.

Be cordial and courteous.
Behaving politely and courteously at your first coin exhibition will enhance your experience. Talk to a dealer and identify yourself when you're ready to look at some particular coins. Request to inspect any coins in his or her display case with civility. You want to come across well at first, so try to create eye contact and use a kind tone of voice. Everyone values your thoughtfulness.

Do not hesitate to ask questions.
You can't learn enough about coins without going to a coin exhibition, so don't be timid about asking questions. What exactly do you sell? Do you have any areas of expertise?"?"
Which of your products is the most popular? Because a curious collector could become a paying customer, most dealers are pleased to answer such inquiries. Inquire about their knowledge if you are interested in a specific series or genre.

Visit as many tables as possible.
One may learn more about coins and the individuals who purchase, sell, and exchange them by attending a coin exhibition. Relationships are crucial on the market floor. (The French term "bourse" translates to "a place where numismatic items are sold.").

Bring along a loupe or magnifying glass.
A magnifying glass or loupe is the primary device used by numismatists. You can't do a thorough inspection of a coin's surface for imperfections without one. Spend some time looking at different coins under a loop, even if you're just starting out in numismatics. This is a great step forward for your numismatic career.

Etiquette is Important

For a pleasant time at the stock market, consider the ANA's advice below.:
- Avoid barging in on a dealer and client when they're talking business. Don't bother asking about the coins or their value.
- When you're done with your business, go back to the dealer's table.
- Keep clients from being blocked from a dealer's table.
- Before making a purchase, educate yourself as much as possible.
- Do not go through a dealer's stock looking for the greatest coins and then ask for a discount on those coins.
- Give the seller some room to make a living.
- If a dealer's asking price seems fair to you, don't bother haggling with them. Don't ask for a discount until you're sure the item is priced too much.
- Always get someone else's approval before displaying an item to a dealer or collector for a second perspective.
- Don't buy a coin on the first day of the show only to try to return it on the last because you realized you wanted another one.

Coin fairs are a great opportunity for dealers to showcase their best pieces. Naturally, they are worried about the safety of their investment. As a consumer, one of your responsibilities at a coin exhibition is to put the dealer at ease. So, please don't stow your belongings on the table, including briefcases, bags, purses, and backpacks. Keep your luggage tucked behind your back, over your shoulder, or under your arm while studying a dealer's coin boxes or trays while standing. This will allow you to study coins without having to hold them.

Whenever you sit down at a dealer's table, keep your belongings off your lap and away from the floor between your legs. You hope the store owner doesn't get the wrong idea about your intentions. The "peek and drop" technique is often used by dealers to misplace coins during events. Think like the dealer and act in a way that won't raise suspicion.

Be tidy
Keep note of the box, book, or tray a coin was withdrawn from while you check the dealer's stock to ensure its safe return. whether you plan on buying anything from the dealer, ask whether they sell boxes so you can keep your items safe until the final inspection. You may buy what you need and send the rest back to the vendor to be put where they belong.

Buying and Selling Coins: Suggestions

If you want to purchase or sell coins from dealers, you'll have more leverage if you know how the market works behind the scenes. One of the biggest issues I see in the coin-collecting business is the huge discrepancy between what the typical customer wants and what the average dealer thinks he should provide that customer. Trust issues are at the root of most of these disagreements.

The typical customer expects the coin dealer to fairly value his coins and pay a good price for them. The typical dealer will pay as little as possible for coins in order to maximize his profit, and the onus will fall on the buyer to undertake his own due diligence. With the knowledge you've gained from this article, you'll be in a lot better position to negotiate with coin dealers.

Best Places to Purchase Coins

The most appropriate place to buy coins is contextual, based on the coins you gather and how you get them. When some people realized there was something interesting in their spare change, they started collecting them. Some people start coin collections because they were given coins as gifts. Furthermore, some people are introduced to coin collecting by a friend or family. You'll have to go out and acquire coins to round out your collection no matter how you get started.

Almost every coin collector has fantasies of becoming rich by selling their collection. You may learn and plan your way to success in this endeavor. But those expecting to make a fast buck are often let down. You'll have more luck as a day trader on the New York Stock Exchange than you would if you tried to make a dollar by tossing

coins. If you follow this advice and just acquire the coins that really excite you, you'll never have to worry about selling your collection for a profit.
You can get coins from anybody, but it's best to be careful. You might overpay or be scammed if you focus too much on finding the best deal. It's important to take your time and not rush into coin collecting. Every coin collector makes at least one mistake in their collection, regardless matter how much time they spend studying their acquisitions. Over time, a savvy coin collector will correct their errors and amass a collection of greater value.

New collectors of coins
There comes a time when you can no longer buy coins at face value to add to your collection. If you're just getting started with coin collecting, it's recommended that you spend no more than $20 at first. You won't lose too much money on your coin collection if you make a mistake. Nonetheless, see setbacks as stepping stones to future success. Consider the motivations behind your coin buy. When I was sitting at the coin dealer's table, did I miss anything? Was I in a rush that wasn't necessary? What stopped you from making a wise buy, if anything?

Most beginning coin collectors spend less than $100 on their first purchases. The value of the coins you're after will rise in tandem with your experience and expertise as a collector. The best venues to buy coins are at coin fairs or through local dealers. There, you may talk to many different people that sell coins. Try to choose a dealer that is approachable and who has a good reputation among collectors. You may also find a reliable coin dealer by joining a coin club and sharing your experiences with other collectors.

Education about coin collecting should be a top priority, since you should know the worth of a coin before you buy it. You may also try out new strategies for amassing coins. United States coin collectors often sort their pieces by mint and mint mark. Still, others collect coins from all across the globe, or from antiquity and the Middle Ages. Your demands in coin collecting supplies will change as you learn more about the hobby.
The Internet may seem like a treasure trove of opportunities for coin collectors. But much like in the Wild West, there are plenty of people

waiting to steal from you on the Internet. It's important to use utmost care when buying any currency online. Do not buy coins from an internet dealer you are not acquainted with.

In addition, the United States Mint offers a direct source for collecting modern coins. The mint often has extremely high markups on its coins. Typically, the secondary market is the best place to buy newly released United States coins one or two years following their original issue. American Proof and Uncirculated coin sets, as well as commemorative coins, fall under this category.

The Advanced Coin Collector
The novice collector has been interested in coins for a while and has tried out a few different approaches. They have a plan and concentrate on one subset of coins since that's what they want to collect. They are now expert coin collectors with a keen eye for quality. Coins priced between $100 and $5,000 fall under this category.

A third-party grading agency, like the Professional Coin Grading agency or the Numismatic Guarantee Corporation, should certify and grade these expensive coins. These establishments will guarantee that the coin has been authenticated and graded by a professional. A coin dealer can't possibly know all there is to know about the hobby. You should get to know a trustworthy coin dealer who focuses on your preferred kind of collection.

Finding a local coin dealer that specializes in the kind of coin collecting you're interested in may be challenging even in the biggest cities. As a result, it's possible you'll need to connect with a coin dealer in a different American city. Attending a national coin event, like the ANA World's Fair of Money, may help you find a reputable coin dealer who can guide you toward your collecting goals. Direct purchases of coins from major national and international auction houses are a possibility. Many coins, however, change hands only via "private treaty" deals and are never put up for auction. Find these buried gems with the help of a coin dealer who specializes in the field.

If you're interested in ancient, medieval, or world coins, you may want to consult with a global coin dealer. You may get some help putting together your collection and learning about import and export rules from a respected foreign coin dealer. New York City is host to the biennial New York International Numismatic Convention every January. At this fair, you may compare and contrast several international coin dealers.

The Professional Collector/Investor
Coins are seen as investments by the savvy collector. Usually, coins worth more than $5,000 are involved in these deals. Experienced collectors usually have one or two go-to dealers who look out for their best interests when it comes to buying and selling coins. The coin dealer will listen carefully to your collecting goals and assess the grade of coins you want.

While high-resolution digital photographs of coins might be useful, nothing can replace a hands-on examination of a potential acquisition. Traveling to several locations to visit different coin dealers or coin fairs may be required. If you don't have time to conduct the research yourself, a trustworthy coin dealer can do it for you.

If you're an expert collector looking to add high-quality coins to your collection, building relationships with dealers is essential. The more experienced coin collector may also acquire coins in national and international coin auctions if they so want.

Selling Coins On eBay

It's easy to make a profit by trading coins on eBay. If you want to build a solid reputation and get the best price for your coins on eBay, you need to create an accurate and high-quality listing. You may expect a higher return on your coins if you sell them on eBay rather than at a brick-and-mortar shop or a coin exhibition.

Keep in mind that it costs money to sell coins on eBay. The final selling price is used to determine the listing charge, delivery cost, and final value fee. Furthermore, PayPal has related costs. Carefully consider the coins you want to sell on eBay.

You should learn about coins if you just acquired or inherited a collection. This can assist you to avoid the pitfalls that many first-time coin sellers encounter. Your coin collection has to be in order before you put it up for sale on eBay.

1. Create eBay and PayPal Accounts

It can be done in three simple steps:
- Sign up for a vendor account on eBay.
- Create a PayPal account so you can start being paid.
- Get your eBay listings up and running.

These articles were written by eBay and PayPal specialists to help you become a top-notch seller on eBay and a trusted PayPal user. You may optimize your earnings by selling coins on eBay after you've created an account there.

If this is your first time selling on eBay, I recommend starting with lower-value coins. You may start selling your more precious coins after you've shown yourself a reliable dealer. Furthermore, if you make a mistake, you will keep valuable currency. Get rid of ten to twenty pennies before you move on to dimes and quarters.

2. Be aware of the coins you are selling

To begin, you must choose which coin you will be selling and how much its wholesale value is expected to be. The Gray Sheet and the Blue Book publish the average prices paid by dealers for United States coins. The wholesale market often offers savings of 50-70% off of retail pricing guides like the Red Book and Coin Digest.

Accurate coin grading is essential for discovering your coin's true worth. Using either a digital or paper coin grading guide, you can evaluate your coins with confidence. For the novice and intermediate coin collectors, I recommend Beth Deisher's Making the Grade.

Always grade your coins conservatively. If buyers think the coin has been over-graded, they won't bid on it, which means it will sell for less than expected or not at all. Potential eBay customers also won't have any faith in you. This is crucial if you want to trade or sell rare or valuable coins. A customer's lack of faith in you will prevent them from taking the chance on another expensive coin purchase from you.

3. Exact and Sincere Descriptions

Carefully assess the state of your coin and provide details about it in the listing. Clearly and honestly explain any flaws, such as scratches, dents, surface damage, or anything else that would detract from the item's value. If you provide consumers with an accurate depiction of the coins they will get, they will be more satisfied with their purchases and more likely to offer you favorable feedback.

The value of your business and the trust of your customers might take a hit if a customer discovers that you hid a significant fault in a coin you sold them. Truthfulness is preferable; keeping a client happy is worth more than making a few more bucks by exaggerating a situation.

Use characterizations like these:
- Lincoln's cheek had a little cut on it.
- There is a dark hue over the whole back.
- Shiny, attractive, and functional surfaces
- Corrosion has damaged around a third of the obverse.
- There's a little pinhole at around the 6 o'clock position.

4. Take Superior Images of Your Coins

High-quality, precise pictures are essential if you want to sell your coins for top money. Get a good digital camera and learn how to take excellent pictures of coins. If the scans or photos you provide of your coins are fuzzy or out of focus, potential buyers will be dissuaded from bidding on them.

You can make back the cost of a high-quality camera plus the time spent learning how to operate it by selling coins on eBay. You should use a color scanner in place of a digital camera if neither you nor your subject needs close-up shots.

5. Auction versus Buy It Now on eBay

There are two ways to post items on eBay: auction and "Buy It Now."
With an "auction" ad, the seller may select the minimum starting offer and interested bidders have up to 10 days to submit their bids. The highest bidder wins the auction and the coin. Make sure your initial bid (or reserve) doesn't go above and beyond what the market will bear. People will stop caring about your currency if you do this to them.

You may offer your coins forever at a "Buy It Now" price, knowing that if a customer is interested in purchasing them, they will pay that amount instantly. For the most part, auction-style listings outperform "Buy It Now" ones, at least in my experience.
It's a combination of "Buy It Now" and "Auction". A Buy It Now price may be used in both a Buy It Now and Auction listing. A buyer may make an instant purchase of your listing by selecting Buy It Now. As soon as a bid is put in, the Buy It Now button disappears and the auction begins. Don't try to make a ton of money by setting the Buy It Now price too high. If you want to sell your item quickly without losing money, choose a fair Buy It Now price.

6. Shipping Cost

Offering "Free Shipping" on coins worth less than $10-$20 will attract more bidders. For coins costing between $20 and $200, the shipping rate, which includes tracking and insurance, is affordable. Coins worth more than $200 should be sent through insured registered mail at a rate that accounts for the higher shipping expenses. Buyers will go elsewhere if you charge too much for delivery, and you'll lose sales.

Special Shipping Considerations for Coins

Coins are constructed of metal, yet even so, the coins may suffer surface damage during transport. Coins should be stored in a non-PVC coin flip or a 2x2 cardboard container for safe transport. Use a Ziploc bag to keep the coins dry for transportation because of the tough conditions. Put them in a bubble envelope for extra safety. When sending coins, never use a regular business envelope.

Coin flips and cardboard holders may be purchased from any coin dealer online or in person. Seal the envelope shut to prevent anybody from opening it in transit. If you want to transport your money in a box, be sure to tape up all of the seams to stop criminals from stealing them.

CHAPTER 5- CARE ABOUT YOUR COINS: PRESERVE, PROTECT, CLEAN, AND STORE YOUR COINS

A cardinal rule for all coin collectors is to avoid creating deterioration or introducing substances that could create spots or color changes. Avoid direct physical touch with your coins whenever possible. This means not handling the coins with your bare hands. Fingerprints are the mortal enemies of collectible coins. It is also essential to prevent coins from encountering one another, as this might result in nicks and scratches. Remove coins from their storage containers only when required to prevent their destruction. Please note that displaying a coin to your acquaintance is not required!

Uncirculated or Proof coins should only be handled by their edges, as even the tiniest fingerprint might lower their grade and, thus, their value. Proof coins have been struck two or more times with polished colors on a similarly polished planchet; they are legal currency. The United States government packages uncirculated mint sets for sale to coin collectors. It is recommended to pick up valuable coins by their edges while wearing cotton or medical gloves. A face mask is also recommended to avoid the formation of unsightly spots caused by moisture particles. Never sneeze or cough near coins, as this can leave marks and damage them. If you believe these safeguards are unnecessary and excessive, be prepared for your coin collection to be destroyed by time without your knowledge. Sadly, I am acquainted with coin collectors who grossly miscalculated the impact of external circumstances on their coin collections, resulting in wrecked collections.

Mint Coins

Coin holders provide adequate protection for everyday use. If you must remove the coin from its holder and set it elsewhere, place it on a clean, soft surface, like a velvet pad. It is an indispensable surface for handling expensive numismatic objects. For lower-value coins, a clean, soft cloth may be used. To avoid scratching any surface, avoid dragging coins across it. Even wiping with a delicate cloth might result in scratches that impair the item's value.

Care and Cleaning of Coins

While it is desirable to maintain a clean environment, it is recommended not to clean the coins. A bright coin may be appealing, but a collectible coin's original appearance must be preserved. Cleaning the coin might considerably lower its numismatic value. There are only a handful of ways to enhance the appearance of a coin. You might harm it rather than improve it.

Collectible coins' value and cost are impacted by unnecessary cleaning. The patina on a coin develops through time and is an integral component of its complete essence and history, reflecting a far greater value than its face value. Eliminating it can reduce its value by as much as 90 percent! Hoarders value coins based on their attractive patinas, which protect the coin's surface. As with the restoration of any art piece, experts must clean coins. They are aware of the best strategies to utilize to maintain the coin's value. If you believe a tarnished coin, you have just uncovered needs cleaning, STOP! It is not a wise decision. It is best to leave the coin in its current state. The observed color change results from a natural process known as toning. And if allowed to develop spontaneously and create desirable outcomes, it can occasionally increase the currency's value.

Toning is caused by the chemical reactions of atoms on the coin's surface, typically with sulfur compounds. It cannot be reversed, but "dips" can remove molecules from the coin's surface. However, only professionals should perform this task. When cleaning coins, you have acquired, discovered, purchased, or inherited, you must adhere to numerous rules.

Never clean a coin whose numismatic value you do not know. If you are unsure of its value, you should not clean it. It is ideal to leave coins in their original condition. Erring on the side of conservatism is better than wasting the coin. Use holders designed for the purpose. Do not attempt to alter the condition of coins, as collectors and dealers favor them in their original form. Most likely, cleaning will cause more harm than benefit.
Because you are not permitted to clean coins alone, you must bring them to a professional coin-cleaning service. Most employ a process

called "dipping" to clean coins without diminishing their value. This is essential, especially if the date and details of the coin cannot be confirmed due to corrosion. A specialist will be aware of how to prevent or reduce further coin damage.

If you must clean a recovered coin, choose the least damaging procedure possible. On the coin, do not use harsh chemicals, sulfuric acid, polishing cloth, vinegar, abrasive pastes, or gadgets that produce a smooth and shiny finish. Before high-value coins, try out coins with a lower value.

Cleaning is a major concern in coin collecting; thus, if you sell a coin, you know it has been cleaned and must provide this information to the buyer.

Best Method to Clean Dirty Coins?

Although you should try to avoid cleaning your coins whenever feasible, there may be instances in which it is required. There is a simple way to clean coins at home if you cannot take them to a professional cleaner. However, you should attempt to clean only circulating coins on your own and wait to have other, more precious ones cleaned by a professional until you can access one.

The most important thing to remember when cleaning coins is to use a gentle touch. Never brush or vigorously rub your coins since such rough motions might be abrasive. Additionally, avoid touching the coin's surface and only touch the coin's edges. Gather your cleaning supplies beforehand so you don't have to search for them throughout the washing procedure and risk recontamination your hands. Before handling the coins, assemble your containers, soap, distilled water, and towel so that the entire cleaning process runs well. Once you have the necessary materials, follow these 10 steps to securely clean coins:

1. Wash Your Hands

It is essential to wash your hands with soap before handling your cash. If you do not, the dirt, grease, perspiration, or other particles on your fingertips could transfer to the coin. Once on the coin, these substances may generate unattractive blemishes or cause the coin to deteriorate. To ensure your safety, wear gloves when cleaning coins.

2. Put a soft towel down.

If you arrange a soft towel on your washing surface, it can be a convenient spot for your coins to dry and a safety net in case you drop one. Folding a soft cloth or towel a few times before placing it on the ground can offer additional padding to your workspace.

3. Prepare a Bath with Soap

Fill a small plastic container with sufficient warm water to completely submerge a coin. Squeeze a small amount of mild dish detergent into the container and let it foam for the cleanser. Use a plastic container for this stage, as a harder surface, such as glass or metal, could scratch the coins. Tupperware and other disposable food containers are ideal for this aspect of coin cleaning.

4. Prepare the Final Rinse

Use a second small plastic jar to store distilled water for the final rinsing of the coins. For this phase of the process, distilled water is essential. Most treated water contains fluoride, which may create a chemical reaction with coins containing several metals. Make every effort to utilize distilled water for this stage, but hot-running tap water can suffice if you cannot obtain it.

5. Clean Your Coins with Care

One-by-one is the finest technique to clean ancient coins. Putting them all in the container at once could lead them to scrape against each other and become injured. To begin, take a penny and submerge it in warm water. Gently rub the coin between your fingers, taking special care to move any dirt, grime, or residue from the coin's center to its edges. Working in this direction, you can use your thumb to remove dirt from the coin's edge.

6. Rinse Your Coin

After washing the coin with soapy water, rinse it under warm running water. When beginning to rinse your coin, remember that you should never scrub. Instead, lightly rub the coin until any soap residue is removed from its surface. Move the coin quickly under the water's stream to dislodge any leftover grit while holding it by its edges. Instead of cleaning the coin, using your hands may wind up grinding the dirt deeper into the surface and damaging it.

7. Carry out the Final Rinse

Again, holding the coin by its edges, swish it in the distilled water to remove any contaminants the tap water may have left behind. If you want to ensure that all potential contaminants have been eliminated from your coin, immerse it in vinegar for approximately one minute after exposing it to tap water.

8. Allow the Coin to Air-Dry

After the coin has been washed, place it on the towel or soft fabric you have prepared. Ideally, you will have rinsed the coin with distilled water or vinegar, and you can let it air dry. If you must rinse your coin with hot tap water, pat it dry gently to prevent spots. In this instance, use a soft cloth towel or lint-free tissue and pat rather than rub.

9. Continue the Cycle

Continue washing your remaining coins one at a time until they are clean. For a particularly dirty coin that requires additional soaking, place it in a separate container off to the side so that you do not damage other coins by placing them in the same container.

10. Store Safely

Before storing your coins, ensure they are completely dry to prevent moisture damage. Place them in a safe location and only transfer them by touching their edges.

Cleaning Diverse Coin Varieties

Even though we've only touched on the fundamental rules you should remember when cleaning coins, you'll find a list of coin-specific cleaning suggestions below. Uncirculated coins should never be washed since they will destroy their mint brilliance.

- Gold Coins should be cleaned with care in clean, lukewarm, frothy, filtered water using a cottony fiber wash-down fabric or a simple toothbrush. Because gold is smooth metal, you must take special precautions to avoid disfiguring or scratching it.

- <u>Silver Coin</u>: Valuable silver coins should not be cleaned under any circumstances. Some silver coins' blue-green or violet tarnish, dirt, minerals, or other remnants improve their beauty and should be left alone. Dark silver coins must be cleaned with ammonia, rubbing alcohol, vinegar, or acetone-containing nail polish remover. Do not polish or rub them.
- <u>Copper Coins</u>: Grape oil may be used to clean copper coins if that becomes required. In such case, olive oil will do just fine. Never touch their flesh with your bare hands. The advantages may not appear for many weeks or perhaps a year, so please be patient.
- <u>Nickel Coin</u>: These coins should be cleaned with warm, soapy, distilled water and a soft toothbrush. When cleaning heavily soiled nickel coins, dilute ammonia with distilled water 3 to 1.

How to Safely Store Coins

You must properly keep your coins to avoid scratching them and diminishing their numismatic worth. The appropriate type of holder must be used depending on the value of the stored coin. You can purchase folders and albums to organize your series or type collection. The presence of sulfur or other compounds in the paper can produce a reaction that alters the color of coins.

Mylar and acetate are excellent materials for long-term storage, but because they are rigid and brittle, they can harm a coin if not placed and removed with care. "Soft" flips were once made from polyvinyl chloride (PVC), which degraded over time and caused severe damage to the coins. PVC gave pennies an emerald appearance. PVC reverses are no longer manufactured or sold in the United States.

If not moved, tubes may carry multiple coins of the same size and appear ideal for most distributed coinages and higher-quality coins. Use hard plastic carriers for more expensive coins, as they do not contain toxic substances and can prevent coins from scratches and other physical damage.

Coins For Collection in Their Cases

Slabs give excellent protection for more expensive coins; therefore, you may want to utilize them. Individual coins are stored in slabs, which are hermetically sealed, hard plastic containers with a hermetic seal. One disadvantage is the associated cost; you will need easy access to the currency in an emergency.

A dry atmosphere with minimal temperature fluctuations and low humidity is important for long-term storage. You must limit your exposure to damp air, as it causes oxidation. Reducing oxidation may not diminish the coin's value but will make it more attractive. Silica gel packets must be placed in the coin storage area to manage ambient humidity.

Even if your collection is stored in a safety deposit box, you must routinely inspect it. Problems may arise if items are not stored properly, but you can act before severe harm happens.

Protecting Your Collection from Theft and Fire

There will always be a risk that your properties will be destroyed by fire or stolen. However, like how you would protect your home or vehicle against pests, there are steps you can take to decrease their presence. Remember that most homeowners' insurance policies exclude coverage of coins and other numismatic artifacts. Typically, a rider is available for an additional premium cost.

In addition, you can obtain a separate policy. Consider joining the American Numismatic Association (ANA), whose members receive coin collection insurance. Ensure that your collection's catalog is stored separately from the coins. Notate where each coin was acquired, its condition, and the sum you paid.

Taking close-up images of each coin individually is also a good idea. For this reason, consult a competent appraiser who uses a Blue Book or Red Book. The insurance company will require the appraisal's documentation.

Theft, fire, dust, water, and other natural conditions that could damage your belongings are defended against by safes. They offer reasonable security for your coins. Some safes provide enough protection against fire but are inadequate against theft. Some safes discourage burglars, but they are not fire-resistant. Fire can damage or destroy your collection even if the flames do not touch your coins. They may melt due to excessive heat.

Another consideration while storing coins in a safe is the humidity level. A high concentration will promote oxidation, which is detrimental to the coins. 30 percent relative humidity is the optimal level (RH). The relative humidity within the safe depends on the surrounding relative humidity. Thankfully, most modern safes are well-insulated and designed with solid seals. Silica gel packets can aid in humidity reduction.

Consequently, if you choose to store your collection at home, you must invest in a home safe that provides sufficient security against fire, humidity, and theft. Ensure you take precautions to prevent or deter a burglar from entering your home. Strong locks and adequate illumination are recommended. Ask law enforcement officers for further helpful advice.

One strategy to protect your investment against theft is to conceal the fact that you are a coin collector. The personal information you provide to numerous individuals may eventually reach the incorrect person. It may be helpful to have all promotional materials relating to numismatics addressed to a post office box instead of your home.

CHAPTER 6: YOU'RE NOT ON YOUR OWN!

This book was written to guide you from the beginning. It is meant to give you basic, fundamental, and advanced knowledge about being a coin collector. The detailed steps, advice, and strategies will guide you on a successful coin-collecting career.

I hope reading this book has prompted you to consider how and why you wish to begin coin collecting. I have created a few pages that detail the three most prevalent sorts of coin collectors to aid you on your quest.

Common Coin Collector

The most common collectors or impulsive collectors. You belong to this group if:

- Regardless of your age, you have a collection of coins.
- You assembled without a specific plan.
- You do not spend an excessive amount on coin maintenance or purchases.
- You may come across outmoded, flawed and coins that are no longer in circulation.

Types Of Coin Collectors

Their natural homes include coin shows, auctions, coin shops, and flea markets; nonetheless, surprisingly little is known about these creatures as a whole. It seems like it belongs to the biological clan of collectors, which includes, without a doubt, humans. To our knowledge, this is the first effort at classifying the nine different types of coin collectors.

Most coin collectors are men. For every thousand male collectors, there is maybe one female collector. No one has offered a logical explanation for this phenomenon. For this reason, let's try to unearth one by probing the dim depths of history. The guy is like a caveman on the prowl for the one coin he needs to complete his collection. He longs to go out in search of his food, track it down, and dispatch it before bringing it inside. What happens next doesn't concern him at all. The penny satisfies his need for hunting, so he places it in a box with many more pennies.

The thrill of the hunt is more important to him than the actual object itself (contrast this person with the Self-exposer, the Researcher, and the Historian).

Even though every coin collector would strongly disagree, there is no true value in collecting coins. Let us take a look at our prehistoric history, which has been with us mentally since the Stone Age. The male would bring the game inside, but the lady would be the one to put it to good use. She divided it up into useful and discarded pieces. This may account why so many women keep putting practical concerns first.

As a result, they won't start collecting coins. As was said before, there is no useful purpose to collecting. Coins aren't very eye-catching since they can't be worn as jewelry, utilized as a fashion accessory, or shown as a valuable asset.

The Classic Hunter

Even though all coin collectors are hunters, the traditional hunter is easily identifiable. The Classic Hunter may be identified by the fact that he always has a list with him when hunting. The collection would be impossible without this list of probable targets. He is solely interested in the coins on his list and will ignore anything else. When he shops, he doesn't care what he ends up purchasing. The act of checking items off a list brings him great satisfaction. Nothing is more satisfying to a Classic Hunter than a full tick sheet.

For the Classic Hunter, there is a mysterious fascination to each of the recorded locations. There, he can make to-do lists with ease. However, a contradiction rules his existence as a collector. Even if he strives for finality, the moment he achieves it, his accomplishments become meaningless. When he finally finishes everything, he plans to sell his coin collection to a dealer. His now-complete collection no longer excites him and instead gives him the mundane pleasure of ownership.

The Classic Hunter has a remarkable capacity for friendship. Being an introvert, he would rather go hunting by himself. Because he lacks an understanding of the background of his coinage, he is reluctant to talk about his work.

The Speculator

Many enthusiasts hope to one day make a killing on the sale of their coin collections. The Speculator has based his collection on an aspiration he has. He thinks a coin's future value increases are its most important quality. The Speculator has bought into the myth that there is gold at the end of the rainbow. By using his wits, he hopes to uncover these treasures. As a result, he treats price lists of relevant coin journals like stock market bulletins and studies them thoroughly. He pays little attention to places where there are no established pricing lists. The Speculator is now widely available online. He is driven by the desire to make a large profit from the sale of his goods to an unsuspecting third party.

Because they cut into his earnings, the Speculator despises dealers. The Speculator prefers to keep a low profile in social situations, letting on that he is a coin collector only when he is very proud of his most recent windfall. Anyone he's talking to my only finds out that the coin he bought and sold made his money if they pay close enough attention.

The Speculator continues to lose money in the long run while exchanging coins. Since he has no idea what the fair market value of a coin is, he has no choice except to congregate in areas where other Speculators are bidding up prices. When market speculation dies down, the price falls to a point where serious collectors may get back in. For a certain time, the Speculator is a collector in perpetuity. As soon as he figures out that collecting coins is a losing strategy, he gives up.

The Aesthetician

The Aesthete seeks to hold in his hands a coin representing perfect art. He could care less whether the price is a dollar more or cheaper. Regardless, he can afford it. Most people who value beauty also value financial security, hence most doctors and pharmacists are aesthetes. The coin market is too noisy and chaotic for the Aesthete, and the Internet is too disgusting! If possible, the Aesthete prefers to shop at auctions in Switzerland. At auctions, he and his lovely wife delight in sporting their finest suits and ties.

There is more than just a person's collection that might identify them as an aesthete. Their very existence is often a creative endeavor.

Their homes, which are all decorated in the same style, go well with the high-quality red wine and multi-course meals they serve guests. Associating with an Aesthete is a pure pleasure. He's not motivated by anything dire. He sees collecting as a means to an end, and he has little interest in coins other than as a means to that end.

The Aesthete only includes countries in his collection that mint the most beautiful coins. Included here are ancient Greek coins, Renaissance numismatic masterpieces, and even modern Romanesque bracteates. But if the Aesthete is taken with an item's aesthetic value, he will buy it regardless of whether or not it has any practical use in his line of work.

The Perfectionist
The Perfectionist takes a more serious approach to his collecting than does the Aesthete. The Perfectionist is completely obsessed by his goal to achieve perfection, as are all others who strive for it. For the perfect coin, he looks everywhere. The condition, look, and location of it is all crucial. A missing tip of the Roman she-tail wolf's tail on the flan caused a collector to part with an otherwise immaculate coin. The Perfectionist does not care about finishing things. Like Caesar, who would have preferred to be the first man in hamlet than the second man in Rome, the Perfectionist would rather have one coin that perfectly represents his beliefs than several coins that fall short in some way.

The perfectionist spends a lot of time thinking about how the finished product should look. All of the most important auction catalogs in history are stored in his collection. If a certain kind of coin piques the Perfectionist's attention, he may easily remember the first time he saw an example that satisfied his high requirements. Only at auctions can the Perfectionist find the high-quality coins he desires. He spends a lot of time at the preview and knows exactly the coins he wants to bid on. The auctioneer will be overjoyed when the Perfectionist starts bidding since he will stop at nothing to win the item. Two perfectionists might drive up auction prices significantly. Neither side is budging at this point. Many perfectionists cannot afford their taste; thus, logic is thrown out the window, hands are raised repeatedly, and at the conclusion of the auction, the winner is often a loser.

5. The Rubbish Chute

The Rubbish Chute is the antithesis of the Perfectionist. The only criteria for his collection are low prices. Collection from The Rubbish Chute is not limited in time or place. He has the same savings goal as Dagobert Duck: to fill an entire pool with cash. His collection is best understood as an accumulation. Wherever a large number of coins can be obtained at a reasonable price, that's where you'll find the Rubbish Chute. At coin markets, he likes to go through the bargain bins, while at auctions, he's looking to buy coins in quantity for close to face value. In addition, he is now often met in cyberspace.

The Speculator is not to be confused with the Garbage Dump. The Rubbish Chute, in contrast, does not purchase for the purpose of reselling; rather, it acquires coins. The Rubbish Chute, like Fafnir of Germanic myth, sits on his wealth to keep it safe, yet unlike Fafnir, he never has to listen to a coin dealer tell him his collection is worthless. The reading of his will is when his loved ones will experience this shock.

6. The Self-Exposer

For the Self-exposer, the collection isn't as important as the monument he can create out of it. The day he finally gets to display his coin collection will be the defining event of his life as a collector. If he leaves his collection to a museum of coins, for example, he can be named as a patron in the curator's annual report.

If the Self-exposer lacks the courage to do so, he might use one of the following routes: a) He may have an auction in his name for his collection; b) if the quality of the collection is too low, he can still publish it under his name, but he will likely have to foot the bill for printing as no one else will be interested. His headshot, which is featured in the collection, dwarfs the biggest coin in his collection, which is very much in character.

The Self-exhibitor usually doesn't put much thought into his collection's theme. He would rather have someone else take care of him than go through the trouble of selecting coins himself for his collection. As a result, you won't see him very often at auctions or coin fairs. The Self-exposer spends much of his time in the United States, thanks to the country's kind taxes policies that let him fulfill his dream of leaving his collection to a museum or university for posterity.

7. The Researcher
The researcher who publishes the findings of his or her own research is called a "Self-exposer." When a researcher's collection, which contains many previously unpublished objects, is made public, it contributes to the field of numismatics.

Knowledge, rather than physical items, is what the Researcher originally acquires. He often buys coins for less than the cost of the materials needed to properly catalog them. He has a passion for exploring the numismatic and historical ties between coins. The researcher could care less what condition an item is in. On the contrary, nothing brings him more joy than successfully decoding an almost unintelligible writing. The Scientist is in need of funding. He is always on the lookout for new things to buy at bargain prices since he likes categorizing them, which can only be done once for each coin. This is why the Researcher is usually seen at coin markets, where he digs through plates full of coins that are hard to classify and so sold at a bargain. The Researcher always finds a "genuine snip," or a coin that is much more valuable than the dealer is asking for, thanks to his extensive knowledge in the field.

The Researcher, like the Speculator, is in pursuit of a treasure; however, whereas the Speculator is after anything of monetary value, the Researcher is for an explanation to an academic mystery. Scientists are fascinating people with whom you can have lengthy conversations about your subject. To listen to them talk is a pleasure. Even the ugliest coins may become important historical records if we look at them through their eyes.

8. The Local Patriot
While everyone pays close attention to the Researcher, every reasonable person tries to get away from the Local Patriot while he or she can. This is a word for someone who is quite familiar with all the places in his immediate area where he can find anything of interest, but who is unable to generalize this knowledge to other situations. Outside of his field of expertise, he shows little curiosity. The Local Patriot may go into such granular detail about his area that

the audience becomes bored. Coins from his home area or the place in which he grew up are his major focus because of the personal significance they have in his life.

The Local Patriot is a person who needs to change. He is always acting superior and condescending. Because he usually just talks about things that interest him, he finds it easy to know everything. He's deaf, dumb, and unable to listen.

The Local Patriot never buys coins from outside of his specific collecting region. This results in him hoarding all common coins and making it difficult for him to get any more. Despite this, he enjoys going to coin markets and regaling everyone who won't run away from him with the names of the coins he's lately added to his collection.

9. The Historian

Coins are tangible evidence of the past, which is why historians value them so highly. What draws him to a coin is not its condition or visual appeal, but rather his belief that he is becoming a part of history by acquiring it. He is an expert on the coinage of Caesar and Cleopatra. Since the Historian doesn't care how much anything cost to acquire, the prices shown here are artificially high compared to the items' true worth, which is based on factors like condition and rarity.

Islands are a sought-after collectible for historians. Some coin collectors have a small collection (twelve coins or less). Instead, then collecting coins from a certain place, they collect coins with particular names on them. They are really enthusiastic as they show off these few goods to others. Professors of Latin (especially in Latin, Greek, and religion - in descending order) and former Latin students (who have all forgotten the horrible scores they used to get in this subject) are the most likely to be of the Historian collector type.

Historians not only collect coins, but also read historical fiction, see every sword-and-sandal movie in theaters, and torment their families by stopping at every ruin they come across on vacation.

CHAPTER 7: EXPLORING US COINS

There is a multitude of resources available to help newcomers to the hobby of coin collecting get started in what is arguably the world's biggest and greatest coin industry. Extensive research and published guides for every U.S. coin series make it possible for a new collector to join the market knowing next to nothing about coins and quickly become almost as knowledgeable as an experienced collector on any numismatic issue. The U.S. market functions smoothly in terms of pricing. Collectors may join and leave the market with relative ease and low expenditure due to the close proximity of the buy and sell prices for most common U.S. coins. Numerous price guides exist, keeping tabs on wholesale and retail prices and establishing their own. The grading of American coins has achieved a degree of complexity that is unmatched elsewhere.

The 70-point scale allows for fine-grained differentiation across grades, especially at the upper end of the scale where emphasis is strongest. The proliferation of independent certification and grading services has helped to standardize a hitherto exploitable area of the market. Numerous coin marketplaces make purchasing and selling coins an easy hobby for anyone with an entrepreneurial spirit. Collectors and merchants have easy access to the main markets via coin shops, coin exhibits, and major auctions. Coin markets and millions of collectors are now accessible from the convenience of your own home, thanks to the Internet and online auctions. Many retailers that were previously struggling have found success thanks to the rise of online shopping. Hundreds of dealers now provide thousands of coins for collectors to choose from. When consumers search for a certain coin, a digital depiction of the coin appears; they then make their choice, pay with a credit card, and wait for the coin to arrive. What could be simpler or more secure than buying coins from a reliable dealer who has been graded by a renowned grading service?

Understanding The Popularity of U.S. Coins

For several reasons, coins from the United States are highly sought for. Amazing artwork: The United States Mint has issued coins with a wide variety of interesting and visually pleasing designs for over two centuries. Millions of new collectors drawn by the popularity of the 50 State Quarters and the Presidential $1 Coin Programs are evidence that coin collectors respect creative designs. Coin collecting may be a relaxing pastime or a challenging intellectual endeavor; the United States has minted coins in a wide range of denominations and kinds, prices, sizes, and rarities. You may aim high but also remember to center yourself.

It's a frequent misconception that only the rich can afford to collect United States coins, but that's not the case. Ask any kid with a collection of Sacagawea dollars, 50 State Quarters, or proof sets. Coin collecting, like any serious collecting hobby, is enhanced by financial means. If you're keen on commemorative coins, you can get your hands on some right now. The U.S. has them in its possession. Since 1892, the United States has honored a wide variety of national events, people, places, and organizations. You can make a lifelong profession out of collecting if you so want. The United States mints a lot of gold coins, so collectors of the yellow metal may have a field day. Collectors all around the globe flock to buy ordinary U.S. gold coins because their prices are sometimes just slightly more than the value of the metal they contain. Intense trading: Coins may be bought and sold in a wide variety of ways, including in physical retail locations, online, over the phone, and via the mail. Thus, numismatics in the United States is always a bustling industry. You may meet many new individuals and make some new acquaintances at coin club meetings, coin displays, online, in newsgroups, etc. Collectors and experts on coins in the United States and throughout the world often get together to talk about and compare their collections.

Popular American Coins

Washington Quarters

The iconic feature of the Washington Quarters is the depiction of some of the world's most stunning natural and architectural wonders. The popularity of the Washington quarter has increased since the 50 state quarters were first released in 1999. Both professionals and amateurs may appreciate how far they've come in terms of design. You probably already know that silver was used to mint Washington Quarters. These coins had over 90% silver between 1932 and 1964, but now only a small fraction of that amount remains.

These coins were the starting point for the first American numismatists' collections. For their silver content, some people wanted to melt them down. Even while most Washington Quarters aren't worth much now, fans of the series may still enjoy a hobby of coin collecting. The best way to get caught up is to start with the most recent season and work your way backward year by year. Also, if you're feeling very brave, you may start a collection of Washington Quarters from a certain decade.

Kennedy Half Dollars

The 1963-assassinated 35th President of the United States, John F. Kennedy, is commemorated on the Kennedy Half Dollars, which are immensely popular domestically and internationally. The first of these dollars was struck in 1964, the year following the tragedy.

Since this currency is no longer in circulation, it will be more difficult for you to obtain one. Nonetheless, it remains legal tender and is still struck for specific collections. I believe that every coin collector should have one of these commemorative coins from one of the most remarkable eras in history.

Lincoln Cents

The Lincoln cent is one of the most versatile coins in American history. In 1909, the first Lincoln cent was struck. The initial versions of the coin depicted two wheat stalks.

Since the first editions, numerous upgrades and revisions have been made to the coins, and today there are hundreds of variants. Fortunately, some of these versions are now in circulation, so I recommend beginning with those. Because they are considered "common" coins, their value is typically not particularly high, but you can easily find different editions on eBay and other online marketplaces.

Commemorative Coins

It is my opinion that you should give some thought to commemorative coins. The purpose of these temporary coins is to honor and remember a special person, place, or event. In the 1930s, when the US Mint was required by law to issue them, commemorative coins first gained widespread appeal in the United States. Distributors bought them at a premium above face value to resell to customers. But this didn't last long since collectors started griping about speculators distorting the market. The consequence was a decline in the number of commemorative coins issued by the United States Mint.

Even though most of them aren't intended to be spent, the United States recognizes them as legal tender. Some of these items, especially if they are "early commemoratives," might be worth quite a bit of money. Washington Quarters (issued between 1932 and 1998) is a great place to start if you're looking for gorgeous commemorative coins that are simple to locate but not for monetary worth. You may also use them to corroborate an occurrence. Consider the possibility that you may one day say, "I was there when that happened."

Many people have been collecting commemorative coins since the first wave appeared. Coin collectors and even others who aren't interested in collecting coins find commemorative coins to be visually pleasing and sophisticated. After acquiring a taste for coin collecting, you may choose to expand into collecting medallions if you find that you like numismatic tributes. The word "medallion" is often used to refer to many coin types, the most majority of which are commemorative issues. A "medallion" is any metal object, often circular and decorated, that has significance (monetary or otherwise). The main difference between a medallion and a commemorative coin is that the former is not usually considered legal money. Generally speaking, this is true for coins.

Morgan Silver Dollar coins

The Morgan Silver Dollar is a massive dollar coin with the portrait of Liberty on one side and an eagle on the other. Designed by engraver George T. Morgan, it bears his name. It was first minted officially in 1878 and lasted until 1921. The coin is rather ancient. The United States Mint plans to release this coin in 2021 as a special collector's item. This coin was hard to find before the year 2021.
You may take advantage of the fact that it will be simpler to find one of these coins starting in 2021. There are four different mints that have put their stamp on this coinage. Symbol-wise, only Philadelphia is missing. This is not a coin I would recommend hunting out for the sake of history or aesthetics, but it may be a good financial investment. The Morgan Silver Dollar's value has increased dramatically over time, and it still may rise.

The Most Valuable Us Coins

Coin collectors know that the value of different types and mints of coins varies widely. Even though the fair market value of each coin fluctuates based on the price at which a particular mint is sold at auction at any given time, certain coins command enduring interest and value. Following is a list of the five most expensive U.S. coins ever sold and their respective prices.

1. 1794 Flowing Hair Dollar

This $1-denominated coin lacks a mint mark. It was sold in 2013 at the Stack's Bowers Galleries' auction house for $10 million.
According to experts, this was the first silver dollar struck by the U.S. mint and the finest coin of its era still extant. The 1974 Flowing Hair Dollar is historically significant because it was the first dollar coin to be standardized nationwide.

2. 1913 Liberty Head Half Dollar

This $0.05-faced coin lacks a mint mark. In 2013, it was sold at the Heritage Auction for $3,1,000,000. The United States Mint produced a minuscule number of 1913 Liberty Head nickels, making them especially valuable to collectors today. Only five known 1913 Liberty nickels exist, making the coin extremely rare. Two of these coins are housed in museums, while the remaining three are privately owned.

3. 1870 S Seated Liberty Cent

The denomination is $1, and the mint mark is S. In 2008, it was sold for $1.3 million at the Stanford Coins and Bullion auction house. The 1870 S Seated Liberty Dollar is an intriguing coin because there is no official record of its existence, although 11 specimens have allegedly been located. The most valuable Seated Liberty Dollars from the 1870s are those with a mintmark from the San Francisco mint.

4. 1927 D St Gaudens Double Eagle

It has a face value of twenty dollars and a mint mark of D. It was sold for $1.65 million in 2005 at the Rare Coin Wholesalers of Dana Point auction house.

President Roosevelt recalled all gold coins in 1933. This declaration meant that all gold coins in circulation and bank vaults were melted down or converted into gold bars, including the 1927-D Saint Gaudens Double Eagle. About 180,000 of these coins were initially struck, making them one of the lowest mintage coins in the St. Gaudens Double series. Today, they are even more valuable, as it is believed that only 11–15 remain due to the recall.

5. 1838 O Capped Bust Half Dollar

It has a face value of fifty cents and the mint mark O. It was sold for $493,500 in 1838 at the Stack's Bowers Galleries auction house. This coin originated at the same time as the New Orleans Mint, which was the first mint to produce silver coins. It is believed that only 20 of these coins were initially struck, and only nine have survived to the present day, making this coin extremely valuable.

Today's Valuable Coins in Circulation

In addition to valuable coins that are no longer in circulation, numerous coins are still commonly used that are valued significantly more than their face value. If you find one of these coins in your piggy bank, you can likely trade it for significantly more than its face value.

1. 1943 Lincoln Head Copper Penny

The denomination is $0.01, and the mint mark is an S. It is estimated to be worth $10,000. Today, copper pennies are the norm, but this was not always the case.

Copper was required for the war effort in 1943, so it was not used to create coins then. Instead, most pennies were made of steel and coated with steel to make them appear shiny. Despite this, a copper batch was produced by accident. Since very few copper pennies left factories during this period, those that did could be worth up to $10,000.

2. 1955 Doubled Die Penny

The face value is $0.01, but there is no mint mark. It is estimated to be worth $1,800. Due to misalignment during the minting process, the 1955 Doubled Die Penny is a one-of-a-kind coin with a double image. 1955 saw the release of approximately 20,000 of these pennies, most distributed as a change from cigarette vending machines. Most doubling occurs on the coin's numbers and letters, leaving the portrait of Abraham Lincoln largely unaffected. A 1955 Doubled Die Penny in "extremely fine" condition could be worth approximately $1,800.

3. 1969-S Lincoln Cent with Doubled Die Obverse

The denomination is $0.01, and the mint mark is an S. It is estimated to be worth $126,000. The 1969-S Lincoln Cent with Doubled Die

Obverse is a unique coin because it was the only one ever appearing on the Federal Bureau of Investigation's "Most Wanted" list. At one point, many believed that this coin was a forgery, as counterfeiters Roy Gray and Morton Goodman were at the time producing very similar fake coins that quickly attracted the attention of authorities. Less than one hundred authentic 1969-S Doubled Die Obverse cents were struck, allowing this coin to maintain a high auction price.

4. 1982 No Mint Mark Roosevelt Dime

It has no mint mark and a face value of $0.01, but no mint mark. It is estimated to be worth $300. All U.S. coins bear a letter denoting the mint where they were struck, with the letters corresponding to the names of cities.

The Philadelphia Mint accidentally omitted the letter "P" from the Roosevelt dime in 1982. No one knows the exact number of these distributed coins, but as many as 10,000 have been identified. If you discover a Roosevelt dime without a mint mark, you can get close to $300 for it.

5. 1999-P Connecticut Broadstruck Quarter

The denomination is $0.25, and the mint mark is P. It is estimated to be worth $25.

Due to a manufacturing error, the 1999-P Connecticut Broadstruck Quarter is another example of a state quarter worth more than its face value. The coin is known as a "broad struck" quarter, referring to the fact that it was not properly aligned in the machine during production. Due to this error, even though finding one of these quarters won't make you rich, they are now worth 100 times their face value.

6. 2004 Wisconsin State Quarter with Extra Leaf

The denomination is $0.25, and the mint mark is D. It is estimated to be worth $1,499.

Due to an error that some believe was deliberate on the part of a mint employee, the 2004 Wisconsin quarter is valuable. On the tail side of this quarter, an additional ear of corn was added to the corn cob's base. In Tucson, approximately 5,000 of these coins have been discovered. Depending on the coin's condition, its value can reach $1,499.

7. 2005-P "In God We Rust" Kansas State Quarter

The denomination is $0.25, and the mint mark is P. It is estimated to be worth $100. Many avid coin collectors are interested in state quarters, but "error" quarters can be particularly interesting and valuable.

The Kansas State Quarter with the inscription "In God We Rust" is another example of a mint error that increased the value of a coin. While grease buildup errors do not always increase the value of a coin, in this instance, the error occurred in an interesting location, making the coin more valuable to collectors.

8. 2005-D 5C Speared Bison Jefferson Nickel

It has a denomination of $0.05 and a mint mark of D. It is estimated to be worth $1,265.

If you find a 2005 nickel that appears to have a pierced buffalo on the reverse, examine it more closely. This detail results from a deep scratch on the die used to strike these coins. In 2010, a 2005-D 5C Speared Bison Jefferson Nickel sold for $1,265 at auction, even though most of these coins are not particularly valuable.

CHAPTER 8: WORLDWIDE COINS

British Coins

Various Mints throughout the globe produce unique collectible coins for fans of the hobby. Some coin series across the globe are more well-known for their designs or technological advancements than for the metal purity of their coins. The individuals who mint foreign coins are as different as the countries they represent. Read on to discover more about the incredible silver and gold coins from throughout the globe that we carry, ranging from Australia to Canada.

The British chose to exchange tea for rum, sugar, cotton, and tobacco rather than cash. Despite this, a great quantity of British currency, mostly worthless tokens or counterfeit coppers, found its way to the USA. Private mints in the colonies began producing a wide variety of tokens for use by merchants and for sale to collectors in the 1790s. Talbot, Allum, and Lee's (TAL) tokens are particularly notable among the first group. Many TAL tokens, originally made for the same-named New York merchants, were downsized and used as blanks in the minting of U.S. half cents. Despite its importance to British history and culture, collecting British coins may be challenging for those with no prior experience. To aid coin collectors and anyone interested in the history of these fascinating pieces of currency, this page classifies the numerous types of British coins.

There are many different types and values of British coins. Depending on their weight value, coins from this era were normally composed of either a precious metal or a base metal. For example, silver was used to make half-sovereigns while gold was used for whole sovereigns. The British half-sovereign was also known as a sovereign, despite its "official" designation. The number of coins in circulation in Britain fluctuated throughout time. Learn about the importance of these coins to the British government before you buy them. These coins are collected by a wide range of hobbyists. Among these enthusiasts are those who want to amass a collection of coins from the reign of Queen Elizabeth II or any other monarch.
Some people also like to collect things from certain eras. This suggests that they are specifically looking for coins from a certain

era. If you're exclusively interested in collecting objects from the British colonial era, for instance, you may limit your collecting to the years 1750-1850. Coins from the Medieval period, the Viking era, and the early reign of the Norman King are also noteworthy.

The third group will gather two coins every year after they were released. This is a great way to have some fun while creating something you can show off and control. Some British coins are far more valuable than others, but there are plenty to choose from if you're interested in collecting. There may be a difference in value between two British coins, but you can tell which one is more valuable by looking at the mint mark. The London mint, which is close to the Tower of London, produces coins that are more sought after than those from other mints. Let's have a look at the range of prices at which certain valuable coins are likely to sell. The time it will take to finish your collection may be roughly calculated using these lists. How much British currency do you have on hand right now? Is someone out of the group? Look closely at some of the more well-known ones, which may sell for thousands of dollars.

The most well-known British coins throughout history are included here, along with brief descriptions of their historical significance and present worth.

Half-Sovereigns

1897 Half Sovereign

1914 Great Britain Gold Half Sovereign

From 1661 to 1816 and 1928 to 1948, half-sovereigns were produced. Due to the demise of the Gold Standard, this coin has been minted in extremely limited quantities. Regardless, this coin remains legal tender. This coin would be worth at least $1,500 in current currency, and a red one would be around $10,000.

Sovereigns

Sovereigns were struck between 1787 and 1817, excluding 1793, when they were struck in the Netherlands. Additionally, half sovereigns were produced in 1787 and 1817. With the start of the First World War, the production of sovereigns ceased because they were replaced by paper currency. These coins would fetch a price of at least $2,000 if they were gold or more if they were silver.

Two-Shilling

From 1797 to 1836, two-shilling coins circulated.
The fact that these coins were introduced as part of an interrupted decimalization experiment is intriguing. Due to their rarity, these are among the most valuable British coins, and they can fetch up to $25,000 each.

Shield Pennies
Except for 1689, when no shield pennies were issued, shield pennies were issued from 1684 to 1756. These coins were not issued again until 1929, when they were worth one penny, but they were not struck again until 1948. Many of these Shield pennies are still in circulation and would be worth approximately $100 in current currency if discovered at an antique show or coin shop.

Copper Halfpennies
Copper Halfpennies were minted between 1797 and 1821. They were discontinued in 1821 and not reintroduced in brassy hues until 1928. These coins are worth at least $1,000 in current currency, and a red example is worth approximately $3,000. If you decide to collect

British coins, you should begin your collection with this coin. Not overly uncommon but certainly valuable.

Threepence

Threepences were minted from 1560 until 1931 when the final coin was struck, and the denomination was discontinued. This coin is well-known because other nations have adopted its name for their currency. All these nations are Australia, New Zealand, and South Africa. These coins have a value of at least $200 in current currency and are desirable to collectors due to their rarity. These coins are among the most fascinating of all British coins.

Sixpence

This series is one of the rarest and most valuable in British history, minted from 1670 to 1889, when the last coins were issued until they were discontinued. If you visit a shop specializing in British coins, the proprietor may refer to this coin as a "tanner." This was the coin's original designation. King Edward VI is represented on the coin.

Pennies

From 1489, when they were first issued, until 1971, when they ceased production, pennies have been minted. The value of these alloys is based on their surface quality and individual condition, which could range from $50 to $100 in the current currency. This is by far the easiest coin to locate in the United States. However, most are not particularly valuable, so you must seek the rarest editions.

Modern World Coins

Sometimes people may refer to ancient coins as "gold coins" or "silver coins." However, this wasn't always the case; glass, ivory, and porcelain were all utilized to make coins in the ancient world.

What about modern coins from throughout the world?
There are literally many different coins from the contemporary world to collect. Numerous commemorative coins are produced by mints for the profit of government coffers, and there are other coins meant for circulation as cash or precious metals for trade as bullion. Some people opted for the challenging task of collecting a single coin from each country that issues coins. Your creativity and ingenuity are the only constraints on data-collecting strategies.

Changes in the Utilization of Coins

One of the most momentous events in modern numismatics happened in 1484. Silver coins worth 60 kreuzers were minted by Archduke Sigismund of Austria (in Tyrol) and given the name "gulden groschen," with each piece being equivalent to one gold gulden. Huge silver coins were made in 1520 by Count Stephen Schlik and his brother at Joachimstal, Bohemia. After then, other names were given to the coins, including Joachimstaler, thaler, taler, dalder, and dollar. The scene was dominated by coins with high face values.

Over time, automated coin minting processes replaced those performed by humans. In the end, steam presses made manual and horse work obsolete. European kings consolidated their authority as they expanded their control over a smaller number of provinces. Local mints were common throughout the Middle Ages because they made it easier to distribute money. The creation of money likewise became centralized as a result of this concentration of power. The number of mints gradually decreased as coin production was consolidated in most countries. Coinage was widely used in Europe, Asia, and the Americas at the start of the modern economic period. Other countries joined the modern economic zone after seeing the success of Australia and Africa. India, like Italy and Germany, standardized its currency over time.

Current Innovations

The use of sophisticated technology and renewable energy sources was the first significant development in coinage in the modern era. The next step was a reduction machine, which used a master die model to produce an identical set of coin dies in the correct size. Dates and mint marks began to appear often on coins. The Christian calendar has been embraced by the vast majority of countries, although there are a few holdouts. The availability of new metals meant a corresponding increase in coinage. Numerous alloys such as nickel, aluminum, and others were used. Some of these metals even outlasted their precious metal forebears. In 1933, countries worldwide stopped using gold- or silver-based monetary standards.

There is no longer any correlation between the face value of coins and their market value. We accept the current coinage as payment because we have faith in the government and the economy. Coins in circulation may now even have unique designs because of advances in minting technology. There were coins with six sides, eight sides, and even scalloped edges. It is not uncommon for coins to have a reeded edge, a lettered legend, or a jagged mix of reeded and plain edges. Braille is included on several modern coins. For safety purposes, holograms have been developed. Ringed bimetal coins were widely used after their 1981 debut by the Italian state mint.

<u>Early Modern Period</u>

In general, medieval coins are classified as made entirely by hand, whereas early modern coins are made using hand-operated technology. The technique of production indicates the era to which a coin belongs.

European Currency
Milled coins were first introduced in England in 1662. The pound system of currency was in use there, which included the pound, the shilling, the florin, and the penny. This persisted until the introduction of decimal currency in the 1970s.
In 1586, the modern currency of the Netherlands started when the number of mints was regulated to one per province by the Earl of Leicester, the governor-general of the Netherlands. In 1602, the

States-General standardized currency and coinage. The Kingdom of the Netherlands was formally recognized at the Congress of Vienna in 1815. The Netherlands officially joined the European Union in 2002.

When France adopted the centime-franc monetary system in the sixteenth century, it was the Valois kings who came up with the idea. The Paris mint began using machines to strike coins in 1640, under the reign of Louis XIV. Then came some beautiful gold and silver coins. Decimal money was introduced during the French Revolution in the 1790s, and France adopted the euro in 2002.

Both Italy and Germany are popular among coin collectors because they were partitioned into nations until the late eighteenth century, during which time several of those states issued their own coins. Although there were many problems, the system remained somewhat orderly since coinage was uniform across borders in terms of weight, purity, and denomination.

In 2001, the euro replaced national currencies in 12 European Union member states. This is the biggest currency union in the world. Spain united as a country in 1492. The gold 8-escudo and 8-real coins were the basis of its monetary system and were divided into "pieces of eight" for use as currency. Spain's monetary system was used by the extensive colonial minting network throughout the Americas. Although the system was not destroyed by Napoleon's invasions, it was eventually replaced in the nineteenth century by a more modern one based on the decimal peseta. This method of payment was used throughout the middle of the twentieth century during Francisco Franco's dictatorship and beyond until the introduction of the euro in 2002.

Czar Peter the Great's reign, from 1689 to 1725, saw a dramatic transformation in the structure of the Russian monetary system. The first coins to be machine-struck in Russia were made at the brand-new Moscow mint in 1711. St. Petersburg was chosen as the new home for the mint and its apparatus in 1719. Until the early 1990s, Soviet coins and banknotes were in circulation. After the fall of the Soviet Union, new currencies were created by the newly independent modern nations throughout Europe and Asia.

Islamic Currency
The Islamic monetary system is as intricate as any other. There are widespread coins and rare ones. Various Islamic mints produced bronze and copper coins for lesser denominations, while silver and gold were used for the dirhams and dinars. During what in Europe would be considered the Middle Ages, gold, not silver, was the major coinage metal propelling the Islamic world's economy. Islamic caliphates were unified and prosperous at this time, in contrast to much of Europe's fractured governments. Few coins include anything other than an Islamic statement because of Islamic restrictions banning images.

Many coin collectors are put off by Islamic issues due to the lack of any recognizable imagery and their inability to decipher the Arabic script and calligraphy used on them.

These Arabic inscriptions or phrases may be identified with the help of any number of specialized coin publications. With the help of this guide, you should be able to read most of these coins without any problems. The prices of gold dinar and silver dirham coins are frequently lower than those of their U.S. and current worldwide counterparts.

Coins from China
Similar to Islam, there is no clear medieval era in the history of Chinese money. Yuan, or silver dollars, were first circulated in Fukien Province in 1861. Two years later, with the territory already under British rule, Hong Kong opened its own mint to make coins with a European aesthetic. Canton was the site of the current imperial Chinese mint, which opened in 1889. The yuan (or dollar) was officially designated as the national currency in 1910. This marks the start of modern China. Popular 1930s Chinese coin issues include those issued by the Communist Army. Rareness extends even to numerous coins with modest face values.

In 1955, the People's Republic of China began minting its own currency. Even though Chinese citizens have been allowed to legally possess gold since 2004, the country still prints "Panda" coins made of precious metals.

Early Modern vs. Medieval
Various nations introduced coins manufactured by machines at various points throughout history. This explains why, for example,

English machine-struck coins appear far sooner than their Russian counterparts do. One production technique may be easily identified from another. Check the quality and condition of each coin by looking at it closely.

From the time of the collapse of the Roman Empire until the beginning of the Renaissance, agriculture was the backbone of most European economies. Coins were more in demand as the Renaissance advanced and the modern European economy shifted from a barter to a monetary system. As a result, larger currency denominations were in high demand and silver mining became more significant in locations like Bohemia. Finding gold and silver in the Americas was also very important. The need for coins of suitable purity, weight, design, and size, all of which had to be made from the metals mined, rose as well. Technology now exists to meet this need.

Significant Historical Coins Ever Struck

These five ancient coins are significant for a multitude of reasons. Some memorialize significant historical moments in western civilization's past. Others exhibit aesthetic and technical achievements in numismatics that have not been matched in over 2,000 years. Still, others are so uncommon that only a handful exist today. Continue reading to discover why each of these ancient coins made it onto our list.

The most significant ancient coin is the Brutus "Eid Mar" Denarius from 42 B.C.

This antique coin commemorates the killing of Julius Caesar, one of the most significant events in western history. On the front (obverse) of the coin is a depiction of Brutus, and on the reverse is a pileus (cap of liberty) flanked by two daggers (reverse). These pugio daggers were most likely assassination weapons. One dagger signified Brutus, while the other portrayed Cassius, his co-conspirator. The pileus was a headgear typically presented to slaves upon their emancipation. The cap and daggers symbolized that Brutus and Cassius had freed the Republic from a despot.

Julius Caesar declared himself dictator for life in 44 B.C. Numerous senators dreaded what his full power would imply for the Roman Republic. A group of senators, notably Marcus Junius Brutus and Gaius Cassius, plotted Caesar's assassination just a few months after his proclamation. In 42 B.C., just months before his suicide, Brutus commissioned this coin. Mark Antony, and Octavian recalled the coins to be melted down and reused. Thus, less than one hundred have survived, making this one of the rarest and most significant coins.

The city of Athens' Decadrachm, 460-430 BC

This old valuable coin was struck under the backdrop of conflict. The Greeks had spent the last forty years repelling Persian invasion armies. The renowned Battle of Thermopylae, the Battle of Marathon, and the Battle of Plataea were decisive conflicts. These successes forced the Persians back into Asia Minor from Greece. Without these victories, western civilization's history would appear very different today.

Athens formed a coalition of free Greeks who sought to liberate any remaining Greek cities under Persian domination. They accomplished this triumph between 469 and 465 B.C. In recognition of this triumph over the Persians, the Athenian dekadrachm was struck. Athena, the goddess of Athens, is depicted on the front. The back features an owl, Athena's symbol.

This coin's silver possibly originated from silver mines located outside of Athens. The coin was so valuable that it was predominantly used by the rich. Most Athenians had never seen the coin, and it ceased to be manufactured during the reign of Pericles.

The Decadrachms of Syracuse 400-390 B.C.

The island of Sicily was the center of ancient coin etching throughout the fifth century. The several towns on the island competed to produce the highest quality silver coins. The following three coins are all from Sicily at around the same period.

Some of the best examples of ancient numismatics are found on decadrachms from Syracuse. These ancient coins include the Kimon Decadrachm, Arethusa Facing Head Tetradrachm, Syracuse Demaraeteion Decadrachm, and the Euainetos Decadrachm.

Syracuse was a major political and economic center in ancient Greece. Kimon was a prominent Syracuse engraver. He is credited for designing the illustrated vintage coin. Arethusa, the water nymph, rides in a quadriga (a chariot pulled by four horses) on the front, with dolphins on each side. The four tyrants of Syracuse are symbolized by the quadriga. In the sky above the quadriga, you can make out the Nike logo.

411 B.C. Akragas Decadrachm

The Akragas Decadrachm is one of the most uncommon coins from antiquity. Fewer than ten artifacts from antiquity are known to have survived. It is one of the greatest coins minted on the island of Sicily in the fifth century. These cities began minting silver coins among the earliest.

The coin was most likely struck in 411 BC to recognize the victor of an Olympic chariot race. The front of the coin depicts the sun deity Helio in his chariot. The eagle represents the sky, while the crab represents the ocean below. The coin's reverse depicts two eagles perched over a hare's body.

The coin was most likely intended for commemorative purposes. Due to the amount of silver used in its production, the currency was too expensive to be used in regular transactions.

460 B.C. The Naxos Tetradrachm

Among the greatest and most well-known coins ever made, this one date back to the fifth century B.C. Unlike most ancient coins, which were produced using many sets of dies, this one was struck using only a single pair. The magnificent details of the coin's design make it a standout above all other instances of ancient Greek money.

In 461 BC, when Naxos was reestablished, this coin was minted as a token of the re-foundation. Due to its proximity to rich volcanic soil, the ancient Greek colony of Naxos on the island of Sicily flourished. The city fell to Syracuse in 476 B.C., forcing the Naxians to choose a new home in Leontini. After Hieron's death, they took back their city. The deity Dionysus is shown on the front, while the satyr Silenos is pictured on the back. The picture of Dionysus on this coin is unparalleled in its degree of detail when compared to other ancient coins.

CHAPTER 9: BEST TIPS FOR COLLECTING COINS

Collect What You Desire, Not What You Believe Is a Good Investment

Numerous claims and suggestions on how to earn money investing in rare coins are made every day. Numerous studies suggest that rare coins have better long-term returns than other types of investments. The coins or stocks selected for the study will have some effect on the gains in value and profitability. Coins are very volatile and may make or break a price comparison based on the coins being compared.

Collectors who are really successful know that placing too much stock on the dollars' worth of their coins might detract from the hobby's other benefits. Buddy Ebsen's character, Jed Clampett, on The Beverly Hillbillies, was a real-life coin collector. A coin with several dings is Ebsen's prized possession. He didn't care that the coin's worth was decreasing with each nick. He said he didn't know each nick's background, but he could guess how its target would feel about it. Considering the coin was a $50 Territorial octagonal slug from the period of the California gold rush, he might come up with a variety of fictitious tales about how it came to be in such a sorry shape. One of the lesser-known but vital features of coin collecting that Ebsen had unearthed was the fact that doing research into a coin's history gives it new meaning.

Studying the history of your coins can bring them to life; a common 1864 two-cent piece might come to life as the first money to bear the slogan "In God We Trust," a 1944 nickel with a distinctive composition might become a memento of World War II, and a Carson City Morgan dollar might become a keepsake of the Old West. After understanding the role, a coin played in national politics and history, it becomes more than simply a collection. Buying coins and building to your collection progressively over time might be a wise financial move. As you study a piece of your collection, waves of joy and satisfaction will flow over you.

Set Aims and Delight in Accomplishing Them

If you're fascinated by coins because of their design, history, or quality, collecting them and then analyzing them in detail might help you figure out what you're passionate about. You know what it is that motivates and engages you. It's a good idea to set some preliminary collecting goals; you can always add to or adjust them as needed. Setting goals for your collection can give you direction and ensure you're happy with your acquisition of the perfect coin.

When it comes to coin collecting, everyone has their own motives and stories. The challenge of putting together a really remarkable collection is the one unchanging aspect of the hobby. Some people find fulfillment in challenging situations. If everything you want happens right away, it loses its fun factor. Spending five, ten, or twenty years (or even a lifetime) building a collection is a satisfying pastime. Find out what it is, whether it's quality or quantity, and stick to it. Do you want to find Morgan dollars from every year and mint they were produced in? Maybe you're interested in American coin collecting. Maybe you're curious about Lincoln cents. Numerous options exist, yet none of them is inherently good or harmful. The right coin collection is the one that sparks your enthusiasm.

If you set some goals for yourself, you'll probably find that you like the activity even more. Consider joining the American Numismatic Association and perusing coin catalogs and webpages. Littleton Coin Company is typical of the reliable businesses that can assist you in setting goals and providing all the numismatic and historical facts you need.

Recognize that Rarity is Comparable
Once you know what to collect, the game really gets going. Your hunt for rare coins to add to your collection may now begin. It's important to have some background knowledge regarding rare coins and their values before making any purchases.
For one thing, the concept of rarity is relative. The coins you buy on the rare coin market will nearly always be scarcer than the cash you use to buy them. A coin's worth does not inevitably increase only because it is inherently more durable than earlier ones. While rarity

does play a role, so does market demand for the issue; many examples are worth more or less than their rarity would indicate.

The Jefferson nickel from 1950–D is a great example. The mintage of the 1950-D was the lowest of any Jefferson coin, hence it is quite scarce. The 1950-D is more valuable than the nickel in your pocket or any of the previous generations of Jefferson nickels. However, the 1950-D was heavily hoarded when it was first released because collectors and dealers anticipated a price rise due to the coin's limited mintage. Since hoarding increased the quantity of high-quality 1950-D Jefferson nickels beyond what the mintage would imply, these coins are now available for less than the price at which they would have originally been sold.

Another timeless model is the 1909-S VDB Lincoln. The 1909-S VDB, with a mintage of 484,000, has a higher price than coins with lesser mintages such as the 1844 and 1845 silver dollars, which had mintages of 20,000 and 24,500, respectively. The rising interest in an already astronomically popular subject is to blame for this situation. As a result, there are never enough working examples to satisfy everyone who wants one.

The famous Morgan dollar from 1893-S is the prime illustration of how rising demand may cause prices to rise. With a total mintage of 100,000, the 1893-S was by and away the best year. The 1893-S's price was heavily influenced by market demand. Even though the 1860-D gold dollar was minted in slightly more than 1,500 pieces, collectors place a far greater value on the 1893-S Morgan because of its increased rarity. Therefore, the price is sometimes as high as or more than that of a gold dollar from 1860 or earlier. The same is true when evaluating various Morgan dollars. The 1885-CC may be more challenging to locate in circulated conditions than the 1893-S can. Collectors who require an 1885-CC usually settle for a Mint State example because of the abundance of these coins. The 1893-S doesn't have this choice, and its enduring popularity means that even circulating examples cost more than equivalent 1885-CC examples.

Make vendors earn your confidence

Several factors, like the coin's rarity and price, come into play after you've decided which coin to buy. Authenticity is of utmost importance when buying coins. It is unfortunate that new risks have emerged surrounding the selling of counterfeit coins, despite the fact that professional coin dealers in the United States have taken extensive precautions to assure that they provide only legitimate coins. Caution is needed while using the Internet. Unfortunately, many coins are offered "as is," which might be a sign that they are fake.

You should only do business with established companies that have a history of satisfied customers. You should also find out how the dealer is regarded by other dealers, collectors, and industry experts. If you want to be sure your dealer is in good standing, you may check with the American Numismatic Association. The Professional Numismatists Guild is another example of a professional organization in this field. Any dealer worth their salt would happily provide names of satisfied customers. Investigate them thoroughly; don't just blindly believe them.

Understand Your Dealer's Grading System
Tens of thousands of collectors are disappointed when they find out that the Very Fine gold coin they bought was really graded as Extra Fine. What can we do to prevent this? Use just the pickiest of distributors. Keep in mind that the grade given by a respected grading agency or dealer is only the beginning of the negotiation process.

Strike and visual attractiveness are two further factors to consider. No of the quality or other factors at play, being knowledgeable is the best way to check what the dealer says. As a result, you should learn about grading standards and services as well as research and practice grading on your own. The grading procedures of any dealer or grading agency are difficult to assess. Both the Professional Numismatists Guild and the Industry Council for Tangible Assets have given the Professional Coin Grading Service and the Numismatic Guarantee Corporation their highest possible ratings of "outstanding."

The hobby has made great strides in standardizing grading since the first grading services appeared in 1986. Rare coin purchasers in the modern day may be certain that their purchases have been fairly valued if they have been certified by a reliable third-party grading service.

In most cases, having a coin packaged by a third-party grading firm is helpful, but a discerning buyer still wants to know that the dealer they're doing business with will guarantee the authenticity of the coin they're buying. You should work out a solution with the dealer directly if you purchased the coin from them rather than a third-party grading service. This means that your best bet for safety is to only buy from recognized, professional dealers that have plenty of expertise under their belts.

There are several factors beyond a coin's technical grade that determine its market value. One noteworthy example is the 1891-O Morgan dollar, which may be found on occasion with a crisp striking, and impressive detail. Despite this, two coins with radically different looks might earn the same grade but have wildly different values because of the grading scale's lack of striking strength and lack of sharp detail.

The technical grade does not account for variations in planchet quality, which may be significant for coins like huge copper pennies. You should be prepared to pay a premium for a coin with a desirable condition, such as a 1799 big cent with a flawless, attractive chocolate brown planchet instead of the more common black ones.

Other criteria, like shine quality, surface quality, and things like tone, may be added to these. The hue of coins, especially silver ones, may vary with time, with certain shades seen as negative (gray or even black) and others as positive (added value) by collectors and enthusiasts. It takes years of experience to learn what to expect from a coin. Although 1893-CC and 1895-S Morgan dollars are expected to have bag markings, the 1881-S is expected to be well-struck and beautiful. The buyer may then determine which coins are really exceptional and which are just average.

Work with Businesses That Have Extensive Inventory

Once you've established a good working connection with a dealer, you'll want to check their stock to be sure they have the coins you're looking for. When it comes to selection, quality, and quantity, Littleton is the only game in town in the United States. They have the resources to buy and store coins of all varieties and popularity levels, as well as the knowledge and experience to accurately grade them. By purchasing the likes of the Midwest Mega Hoard, Southern "CC" Cache, Vermont Yankee Hoard, and New York Subway Hoard, Littleton has satisfied the needs of tens of thousands of collectors. This is crucial for purchasers since the coin you want is very certainly already in their inventory, and if it isn't, they'll go out of their way to find it.

Protect Your Investment: Anticipate a Full, Hassle-Free Guarantee
A coin may sometimes let you down. If a business is hesitant to guarantee your money back in full, you should go elsewhere. You should never feel awkward about asking for your money back. The coin-collecting industry has to catch up to how modern customers want to be serviced. You should have at least a 30-day guarantee. If you decide to return a coin you purchased from Littleton within 45 days, your purchase price will be refunded in full.

Be Certain When Purchasing Via Mail
Mail-order is preferred by millions of collectors because of its reliability and security. The arrival of your currency shipment is almost as exciting as the arrival of a brand-new, colorful catalog. Again, deal only with companies who stand behind their products fully, both in terms of warranty coverage and (crucially!) delivery assurances. buying through catalog or online is just as risk-free as buying in shops, at shows, or at auctions, provided you deal only with reputable merchants. You'll make better choices if you have more information to work with.

Protect Your Collection with Storage Products of Archival Quality
Nothing is more upsetting than discovering that improper storage has diminished the value of your coins. Consequently, it is in your best interest to learn about every option. There is a wide variety of options to choose from, including albums, folders, and presentation boxes. If you want your coins to have less of an effect on the environment, you should always choose archival-safe, acid-free materials. The vast inventory of Littleton Coin Company is perfect for long-term storage.

Permit Yourself to Be Carried Away
Authentic historical artifacts are the only item that can really take you back in time. A Lincoln cent struck in 1943 out of a very rare zinc-coated steel alloy; what could possibly be more historically significant? The United States sought to save its copper supply for use in World War II, therefore the 1943 Lincoln cent did not look or weigh like a regular Lincoln cent. Since this rare steel alloy was utilized just for 1943 cents, they are not only unique dates for Lincoln cent collectors but also physical reminders of the cost of winning the world's greatest war. Because of this, the 1943 cent will forever have a special position in history.

Or maybe you have a large cent from 1794 that you believe George Washington carried, or an Indian Head cent from 1861 that you imagine a Civil War soldier used in battle. Coin collection is interesting since there are so many different aspects to explore.
Please take note of these 10 top-secret recommendations so that you may devote more of your attention to the thrill of the search and less to dodging obstacles. In conclusion, take it easy, but don't be afraid to allow yourself to be caught up in the excitement of this fascinating and rewarding pursuit.

Methods To Improve Your Coin Collection

As a dealer who works with collectors of varying experience levels, I am well-versed in the traits that distinguish experts from amateurs. I agree that experience is crucial, but some of the most accomplished collectors I know are amateurs who trust their instincts more than anything else. The following advice and clarifications may help you become a better collector.

1. Avoid Spreading Yourself Too Thin
Many times, I've seen complete immersion in the world of coin collecting among first-timers. An enthusiastic coin collector who spends more than they have and ends up with a disorganized collection is not to be blamed. It's crucial to practice restraint and avoid getting caught up in an "I must have it all" mindset, even if your collecting priorities change over time. Choose a secondary collection (paper money, tokens, circulating Liberty Seated silver) if you can't tolerate the prospect of waiting but still want to satisfy your buying needs.

2. Become an Expert in Your Series.
Those who dedicate themselves to learning all they can about a certain coin series are often regarded as the most accomplished collectors. There might be a few different interpretations of this study's findings. For some, the issue of currency shortage and availability is more pressing. If there is a lack of resources on a particular series of coins, a collector may choose to produce a book or build a website about them. Spending time learning about a series will pay off in spades.

3. Develop positive relationships with at least one or two dealers
The best coin collections are the result of collaboration between a collector and a dealer. When building a collection, look for Type One Liberty Head double eagles and About Uncirculated Dahlonega half eagles. A significant number of good coins will be out of your reach unless you have a reliable relationship with a dealer. You can probably get most of the coins you need via eBay or the blind bidding at a Heritage auction, but I worry that your collection will be more spotty than faultless. Like Amazon.com for books, you may

buy and sell contemporary coins directly from other collectors. But if you're just starting out in the collecting world and believe you can handle a challenging set on your own, you may want to rethink that assumption.

4. Investors Should Think Like Coin Collectors

An old cliché states, "A numismatic investor almost never earns money, but a good collector often does." This proverb is often attributed to Doug Winter. Consider how the coin speculator always purchases undesirable coins from undesirable sources at undesirable periods. They often pay more and earn a profit when trading goods. But collectors acquire coins for their own amusement rather than to resell them, and they often receive a high return on their "investment" even if they don't set out to make a profit. Stop right now if you've been buying coins but have no plans to use them. Get some bullion and liquidate your assets. You won't have to stress as much when it's time to liquidate.

5. Purchase with Aesthetics in Mind

Due to their scarcity, ugly coins should only be purchased by experts. There are a few outliers to this rule. The 1864-S half eagle is so rare and expensive that I would acquire it even if it were hideous. However, if we're talking about an 1864-S double eagle (which is readily accessible and, with patience, may be located with good visual appeal), it would be a horrible error to acquire a mediocre coin.

This ties to the second point noted above; as you gain expertise with your coin collection, you'll have a better idea of how prevalent particular grades are compared to others. You should be prepared to hear many "that's ugly but..." comments when attempting to sell your coins unless they are really rare.

6. Pay More for Quality

Another truism in the hobby is that "excellent coins are not inexpensive, and inexpensive coins are not good." A coin might be had for a reasonable sum these days. It is tough to win auctions or locate financially stressed dealers ready to part with their best offers at cheap rates due to the scarcity of high-quality coins on the market. The simplicity of supply and demand has led to a very simple coin market in the last five years.

There is a sizable audience eager to buy each unique unusual coin. If you are unwilling to pursue opportunities for professional growth, you risk missing out on them or never being given them at all. However, I do not advocate overpaying for coinage. Consider the opportunity effort of passing up other deals, as well as the potential return on investment from the additional funds invested.

7. Rely on Your Intuitions

Not believing my intuition has been the root cause of almost all of my financial missteps. You shouldn't have to force yourself to appreciate it in order to know that it's not the correct coin for you. Unless it's the 1864-S half eagle you've been hunting for since 1998, don't purchase a coin if your investigation reveals it's worth much less than the asking price. A trader is a third possible reliable party. If a man's offer of money over the phone causes the hair on the back of your neck to stand on end, you should probably avoid doing business with him.

8. Learn How to Value the Collections You Have

The vast majority of novice coin collectors overpay or underpay for their coin purchases. Thanks to the online auction values reached in archives provided by PCGS, NGC, and Heritage, most collectors today have no excuse not to know how to evaluate commonly traded coins. Rare coins like our acquaintance the 1864-S half eagle are in a league of their own. This topic is so interesting to me that I often revisit past blogs to refresh my memory.

9. Be Patient!

Let me give you an illustration of why it pays to be patient when dealing with currency. I met a coin collector about a year ago who had a thing for antique gold coins. After I sold him some coins, he was hooked. He wanted me to sell some coins to assist him to come up with the capital for another purchase. He said that he lacked patience and was only accustomed to collecting coins that were simple to get by. Over the course of six months, I searched far and low for the "perfect" coin for him. When I eventually found it, though, it was a home run, surpassing even his greatest expectations. Patience is especially important if you want to acquire rare and/or highly appealing coins in today's market.

10. There's No Point in Learning to Grade

I didn't decide to take a crash course in urology when I developed kidney stones two months ago; instead, I sought out the best physician I could find. And it's unlikely you'll ever become an expert enough grader to discern an MS62 from an MS63. With experience, one can determine if a coin is genuine in terms of its color, surface, striking, age, etc. I once thought it was a good idea to recommend that coin collectors learn to grade, but now I'm not so sure. You can learn to grade coins, but if you really want to focus on anything, choose those in the top five to ten percentiles.

Perhaps some of these concepts are hitting a little too close to home for comfort. This article wasn't designed with anybody in mind in particular, and I've seen novice and expert collectors alike make the same blunders. If you can recall even a small number of these dates, you'll have a much easier time learning about rare coins and will have a far better time collecting them.

Coin Lingo

- Altered Date - The value of an altered coin has been increased after it has left the Mint. The removal of a mintmark or the introduction of a fake are two common examples of such manipulations. The term "altered" is often used to describe cleaned or refurbished coins.

- American Numismatic Association (A.N.A.). Association for the Promotion of Numismatic Education, the Preeminent Non-Profit Organization in the Field. Anyone with a genuine interest in numismatics is invited to join, whether they are experienced coin collectors or just starting out with paper money, tokens, or medals.

- Anglo-American Coins & Tokens - The term "Anglo-American" is often used to describe coins from the 17th and 18th centuries that were predominantly private issues produced in Britain for usage in the American colonies. The United States acquired several British coins and tokens that were originally intended for use in Britain.

- Annealing - Coin planchets are heated just before they are struck so that the design may be impressed more deeply. Advanced equipment is being used to carry out this method. Planchets were annealed in the past using tongs and a charcoal fire.

- Attribution - Attributing a coin to a particular nation, period, monarch, or even year of issue is common practice. The majority of coins can be recognized instantly, either by sight or using a standard reference book. The use of the word "attributed to" in reference to a country, monarch, or other historical figures on a coin is purely attributive and not definitive. Sometimes people's beliefs are based on old reference materials that have never been proven wrong or proven right.

- Average Circulated - A grade given to coins depending on how old they are. A 1900 Barber quarter in "Average Circulated" condition, for instance, would probably be graded as About

Good. Even in "Average Circulated" condition, a 1955 Washington quarter is probably going to be classified Fine or Very Fine.

- Bag Marks - Coins may cause minor scratches or abrasions by rubbing together in bags. Bag marks on uncirculated coins are to be expected during shipping, but the rare date coins that manage to avoid them are worth a significant premium.

- Bar Cent - A token with a bar design on its reverse, indicating it was struck in the United States shortly after the Revolution. The word "USA" is written in script on the obverse of the coin, with no other design or date present.

- Barber Dime, Quarter, Half Dollar - Charles Barber designed these coins as the Mint's head engraver in the late 19th century.

- Base metal - is any metal besides silver, gold, and platinum.

- Bath Metal - Zinc-and copper-alloy metal. This metal was often used for British tokens and medals in the 18th century.

- Bid Sheet - (1) A perforated sheet of paper in an auction catalog that bidders use to keep track of their purchases. This document is then sent to or handed directly to the auctioneer.

- (2) Wholesale sheets used by coin dealers on a weekly, monthly, and quarterly basis are frequently referred to as bid sheets.

- Bilingual - Referring to the dual-language inscription on a coin.

- Billion - A very low-quality silver alloy that contains more than 50% copper. Billion has been used as money, albeit in the form of devalued coins, since antiquity.

- Bit - During the 1700s and 1800s, old Mexican 8 reals silver coins were often used across America. To give you an idea, "two bits" was one-fourth of the coin, and a "bit" was one-eighth. Thus, the name "Two Bits" was given to our quarter dollar.

- Black Book - An updated paperback catalog of United States coin values that is published on a yearly basis.

- Blank - Coin blanks are many names for the same thing: the circular piece of metal that has the same size and weight as the finished coin before it is struck. Blanks used to be cut by hand from a metal coil using specialized shears.

- Booby Head - This version of the 1839 Large Cent looks like it was etched by a clown instead of a professional artist.

- Bourse - A group of coin merchants who set up shop at a conference and sell their wares to attendees at individual tables or booths, thus the term "coin show."

- Branch Mint – The Philadelphia Mint's American counterpart, or any other US mint.

- Bracteate - A medieval European coin so thin that its design may be seen through to the opposite side.

- Broad strike - The diameter of this coin is larger than average. This is not an enormous planchet, but rather a striking fault. Due to the lack of a protective collar, the coin is struck at an angle that causes it to grow beyond its normal dimensions.

- Brockage - A coin with a conventional pattern on one side and a reversed design on the other; sometimes known as a "miss truck.

- Broken Bank Note – Privately printed bills from the 19th century. In most cases, the businesses or individuals that produced such money failed, thus the term "broken bank note.

- Bronze- copper-zinc-tin alloy that contains (usually) 95% copper, 4% zinc, and 1% tin. Bronze has been used for currency from ancient times. The exact formula has changed from time to time and place to place.

- Bugs Bunny - Ben Franklin's fangs protrude like Bugs Bunny's in this cartoonish variant of the Franklin half dollar from 1955.

- Bullion - Bars, ingots, or plates of uncoined gold or silver.

- Business Strike - A coin that has just one side struck, like a regular manufacturing coin, but not meant for collectors.

- Bust - A device comprising the head, neck, and a portion of the shoulder or chest.

- Cabinet Friction - Cabinet wear, also called "cabinet rub," is the rubbing off of a coin's high points by being stored for a long time in an unlined wooden cabinet drawer. Wooden coin cabinets were widely utilized by collectors from the early 1600s through the late 1800s.

- Cameo - Patterns that are embossed or raised. "Cartwheel" refers to a large coin, usually at least a silver dollar in size.

- Cartwheel - A British two-penny coin with George II's portrait, struck in 1797. The two-ounce copper object was unusually thick and heavy for its size, with raised rims on both sides that made it seem like a wagon wheel. Its nickname of "cartwheel" seemed appropriate.

- Cash - The Chinese copper coin with a square hole for stringing.

- Cast Coins - Coins manufactured by pouring molten metal into a mold instead of striking with dies.

- Cent - a unit of currency equal to one hundredth of a US dollar. Centimo in Spain and Venezuela; Centesimo in Italy; Centavo in Mexico and several other Central and South American nations; Centime in France and Switzerland; etc.

- Cherry-pick - The ability to recognize and acquire a less common but more valuable item.

- Chop Mark - (often Chinese) merchant's test mark punched into a coin to determine its weight.

- Circulated - Facilitated access for more people. showing signs of having been passed on from user to user.

- Civil War Tokens - Due to a shortage of currency, unofficial coins were forced into circulation during the American Civil War.

- Clad Coinage - U.S. coins from the dime through the dollar series of 1965 and thereafter. Each coin has a copper-nickel or silver plating on both sides and a copper core in the middle.

- Clash Marks - Part of a gadget or legend is impressed on the die's facing field during the pressing process. This happens when two dies collide with normal coining force but no planchet in between.

- Cob Money - Coins from Spain, Central America, and South America made of rough and uneven silver.

- Coiner - The employee of the mint who stamps planchets to create coinage.

- Colonials - Term used to describe any coins struck in or for the United States before the United States Mint was established.

- Commemorative - A coin minted in honor of a special occasion or person.

- Coppers- is a generic term for copper coins from the late 18th century.

- Counterfeit - False money is an unauthorized copy of a coin.

- Countermark- A countermark, or counter stamp, is a stamp or mark placed on a coin to attest to another authority's use or to signal a reduction in value.

- Crown - The British silver dollar is a silver coin with a $1 face value.

- Cud - A lump found on a coin struck from a broken die.

- Cull - A worn-out or damaged coin. Used not just of coins now in circulation but also of those that have been held by the Mint owing to quality control issues. These materials are sent back to be recycled.

- Data Set - One of each kind of coin produced in a run.

- Denarius - The basic silver Roman currency.

- Designer the artist who created the coin's design. Currency dies are created by engravers who carve patterns into the metal.

- Instrument - Crucial component in construction.

- Coin minting requires the use of a "die," a metal plate with an etched pattern.

- A die crack is a tiny, raised line on a coin that appears when the die breaks during minting.

- Die Defect - A blemish in a coin caused by a faulty die.

- Die variations occur when there is a little shift in the general design of a coin.

- Dime: That's one tenth of a dollar, or 10 cents. A primitive version of "dime."

- Double Eagle: The "Double Eagle" is a United States gold coin with a face value of $20.

- Double Struck: This phenomenon, known as "double struck," is typical in earlier coins and occurs when the two imprints left by the working dies aren't perfectly aligned with one another.

- A die that has been double-hit by a hub or device punch is no longer usable.

- Doubloon: The Spanish-American gold coin called a "doubloon" had an original value of $16.00.

- Drachma: The Greek drachma is the country's official currency. The Roman denarius was roughly similar to a small silver coin.

- Gold Ducats: Gold ducats are circulated in several European countries. This item was formerly a coin from Italy's 12th century.

- Fake Coin: A fake coin made via electroplating, often known as an electrotype.

- Electrum: Electrum is an alloy of gold and silver that occurs in nature.

- Exergue: A coin's exergue is the area around the edge that isn't the main design.

- Field: "Field" refers to the blank space on a coin's face.

- Coinage: Coinage depictions of people whose hair is pulled back in a band around the forehead are called "fillet heads."

- Gold and silver fineness are always expressed as a fraction of a thousandth of a gram.

- A flan is a metal blank of coin size and form. A synonym for planchet.

- The United States regularly circulated paper money in values smaller than one dollar both during and after the Civil War. Various issues were published between 1862 and 1875.

- Gem – This term designates coins that are either Uncirculated or Proof and have been graded as having "imperfection" and "excellent aesthetic quality."

- Half Eagle: U.S. gold coinage called a "Half Eagle" has a face value of $5.

- Trying Times During the duration of Andrew Jackson's presidency (1834-1841), tokens, or pieces of a political or promotional character, were privately created and used as money. They resembled the massive cents used at the time in the United States.

- A hub die is a specialized die that is not used to strike coins but rather to transport designs to working dies.

- The reverse design of a coin, often known as its incuse. A coin's design is said to be "in relief" if it stands out from the flat background.

- A jeton may be thought of as a little medal, token, or currency.

- Laureate: to wear a laurel wreath as a crown.

- Legend: What you see on the front of most coins is the legend.

- Lettered edge: Some foreign and older United States coins include an inscription along the thin edge, which is known as the "lettered edge."

- Maundy money is a special kind of English silver coin issued by the king on Holy Thursday.

- Milled edge describes a coin with a pronounced border around its circumference. Do not mix this with the coin's reeded or serrated edging.

- Erroneous or defective coins produced by a mint due to improper striking.

- Mint luster refers to the "frost" or "sheen" of a "Mint State" or "Uncirculated" coin.

- Collectible coins of a single date offered for sale by the mint in their original Uncirculated state.

- Identical to "Mint State" condition. A coin that shows no indications of use whatsoever.

- Minting refers to the production of coins. The total number of minted coins.

- A coin's mintmark is a mark, usually a little letter, that indicates the facility where it was struck.

- A moneyer is a legal coiner or mint master.

- A coin's motto is an inspirational phrase or statement engraved on the reverse.

- A mule is a coin struck from a combination of dies that were never intended to work together.

- Noltgeld is coins and paper money kept for unexpected expenses. During World War I, Germany printed a lot of them to combat inflation.

- Face: The obverse is the "face" side of a coin, where the date and major design are shown.

- off-center: A coin is said to be "off-center" if it fits into the striking chamber just partly.

- <u>An overdate</u> is a date that has been formed by adding a new number to a die that already has a date on it.

- <u>An Overmintmark</u> is a variant created by punching another Mintmark over the original.

- <u>An overstrike</u> occurs when fresh dies are used to make an imprint on a coin that has already been struck.

- <u>Long-term oxidation</u> of copper and bronze coins results in a green or brown patina.

- <u>Currency</u> that has not yet been widely used; may be of a new design, metal, or denomination; used for trials or experiments.

- <u>The Piece of Eight</u> was a kind of international trade money used between the Americas in the 17th and 18th centuries. It was equivalent in value to today's Spanish-American dollar. U.S. silver dollars' ancestor coin.

- <u>A coin's design</u> is struck into a metal blank called a planchet.

- <u>Proof-like</u> refers to a coin that seems like it was struck from proof dies, but was really struck from a blank that was not proofed.

- <u>Proof coins</u> are those produced from perfectly polished dies specifically for collectors.

- <u>A Proof Set</u> is a group of identical proof coins that are released together by a mint the same year.

- <u>Gold coin</u> with a face value of $2.50; its official name is "Quarter Eagle."

- <u>Coins</u> with such low mintages are considered "rare" by collectors.

- The edge of the coin has vertical grooves that go all the way around it, giving it a reeded appearance. All modern United States silver coins include the rim.

- Relief: The term "relief" is used to describe any design element on a coin that stands out from the flat background. The opposite of relieve is indict.

- Restrike refers to a coin that was produced using the original dies at a later period.

- Reverse: The "reverse" of a coin is the back side, where insignificant designs are placed. Different from what you see on the back.

- Scarce means there are more of the item than would be considered normal for a coin of its kind to be in circulation today.

- The rim is the raised border around a coin that helps to preserve its appearance over time.

- Script refers to unofficial paper currency.

- Siege Pieces are emergency coins created during a siege, often known as obsidional or war money.

- An example of a series is the production of Morgan dollars by the United States Mint between the years 1878 and 1921.

- Paper money and fractional currency in the early United States were known as "shinplaster," a slang term.

- Slang name for a coin that is graded EF or AU but can be passed off as MS thanks to a thorough cleaning and recoloring.

- In lieu of proof sets, the Special Mint Sets were produced between 1965 and 1967.

- A token is anything other than a government-issued coin that has the ability to be used as currency.

- Dollar for International Trade, or "Trade Dollar," was a silver dollar created for international transactions. In 1873, the United States government issued the first trade dollars to promote commerce with Asia. Trade dollars have also been issued by other countries.

- A truncated hemi bust is missing its bottom margin.

- Type refers to a coin's distinctive appearance.

- "Variety" refers to a coin that has different dies from other examples of the same design, kind, year, and mint.

- Wartime Silver - From October 1942 through December 1945, the metal used to strike five cent pieces was a mixture of 35% silver, 56% copper, and 9% manganese.

- Whizzing is the deceptive practice of giving a coin a surface that looks like mint bloom by using a wire brush or any similar equipment.

- Each denomination is released on an annual basis. All of the coins you see here date back to 1990, from the penny to the half dollar.

CONCLUSION

Some collectors put considerable time and money into their collections because they are passionate about what they are collecting. You should treat every large purchase of a collection as an investment and follow some basic guidelines to minimize bother and tax liability.

By planning ahead and following some basic recommendations, you may minimize the financial toll and administrative burden of paying taxes without breaking the law.

Investing In Coins

Investing in coins: yes, or no? Many others, including me, say "no." Misinformation and exaggeration have plagued the rare coin investing market for the last four decades, just as they have every other investment industry. Many wealthy people have earned their wealth by investing in rare coins, despite the fact that the value of coins is subject to boom and bust cycles just like any other investment.

Investment (whether in coins, stocks, or your cousin's Internet startup) is a complex matter, much beyond the scope of this book. In the last few years, there have been two comprehensive statistical analyses of coins as investments. The original research, published in the Journal of Financial Planning in August 2005, was written by Dr. Robert Brown, a certified financial analyst. According to Brown's research, investing in U.S. coins yields a 9.8 percent compounded rate of return over 30 years.

There is just one other study on this subject that we are aware of, written by Neil and Silvano DiGenova and published in 2007's The Investor's Guide to United States Coins (Coin & Currency Institute). The coins in the portfolios under scrutiny were all hand-picked by numismatist DiGenova and included in his recommendations published over two decades ago. Dr. Jason Perry of the Federal Reserve Bank of Boston oversaw this research project. Rare coins in the DiGenova portfolios, he and Neil calculated, generated a 9.5% compounded rate of return over the same time period with the lowest risk of any investment of similar volatility. They backed up their claims with proof. These return rates have turned out to be on the bottom end of the statistical range since the market has gained considerably after the research was done.

For those looking to speculate or diversify their holdings, coins are a good option. The rare coin market has seen some dramatic fluctuations over the last two decades, suggesting that investors who purchased low and sold high may have earned a tidy return. In Chapter 7, I detailed the rarest and most precious coins now in circulation, as well as a few rare examples of incredibly costly coins that saw far higher prices the second time they hit the market, even if it was just a few years later. Similarly, depending on what you bought, you may have taken a major loss if you invested in coins at the market's high in 1989.

Find a coin dealer who specializes in investments if you're thinking about buying coins. The pros and downsides of investing in rare coins are beyond the scope of this book. Investing in coins is a risky business. However, the coin investment industry has been around for approximately four decades, and it is thriving right now.

Printed in Great Britain
by Amazon